CHALLENGE AND CONTINUITY

I0894072

CHALLENGE AND CONTINUITY

A Study of Rabbinic Responses to Modernity, Science and Tragedy

YONI BIRNBAUM

VALLENTINE MITCHELL
LONDON • PORTLAND, OR

First published in 2017 by Vallentine Mitchell

Catalyst House,
720 Centennial Court,
Centennial Park, Elstree WD6 3SY, UK

920 NE 58th Avenue, Suite 300
Portland, Oregon,
97213-3786 USA

www.vmbooks.com

Copyright © 2017 Yoni Birnbaum

British Library Cataloguing in Publication Data:
An entry can be found on request

ISBN 978-1-910383-39-1 (Cloth)
ISBN 978-1-910383-40-7 (Paper)
ISBN 978-1-910383-41-4 (Ebook)

Library of Congress Cataloging in Publication Data
An entry can be found on request

All rights reserved. No part of this publication may be reproduced in any form or by any means, electronic, mechanical, photocopying, reading or otherwise, without the prior permission of Vallentine Mitchell & Co. Ltd.

Printed by Edwards Brothers Malloy Inc, Ann Arbor MI

בעזהשי"ת

לז'נ
ר' יעקב יוסף בן צבי זאב ז'ל
ומ' שינא בת מרדכי הלוי ז'ל

In Everlasting Memory of Sonia and Jack Birnbaum

A special couple who instilled a deep sense of commitment to the continuity of Jewish tradition in their children, grandchildren and great-grandchildren.

Dedicated by their sons Wayne and Simon Birnbaum

Contents

Preface

One of the most critically important aspects of spiritual leadership is the ability to understand, empathise and respond to the particular issues of the day. A spiritual leader who fails to fully appreciate the nature of the challenges facing their particular community risks being perceived, at best, as outdated, and at worst, as insensitive and irrelevant. Conversely, leaders who are able to draw upon the wisdom of their faith in order to provide guidance for those seeking a spiritual pathway through the complexities of the age have arguably performed the greatest possible service to their followers.

Whilst this is true of any faith, and of any form of spiritual leadership, it is particularly true of traditional Judaism and the expectations of its rabbinic leadership. Dating back to early antiquity, one of the central roles of a rabbi has been the ability to analyse critical issues of the day and provide an appropriate response, drawing on the depth and breadth of Jewish tradition in order to do so. Thus, the Torah itself sets out the basic requirement to 'enquire' of the 'Levitic Cohanim',[1] possibly the earliest form of rabbinic leadership, when matters of doubt in Jewish law arise.

Nor has this traditionally been limited to areas of Jewish law or halakha alone. Philosophical, ethical and moral questions, as well as appeals for guidance in times of crisis, have all come the way of the rabbi. Yet, the methodology employed in responding to these queries has followed a distinct and continuous pattern over the generations. Great weight is given to both precedent and community tradition as well as the views of earlier rabbinic scholars when formulating responses.

This work seeks to highlight a variety of rabbinic responses to some of the particularly critical issues presented by modernity and science, as well as spiritual leadership in the course of the tragedy of the Holocaust. It will also seek to establish the continuity of the methodological principles utilized in rabbinic responsa, through a focus on the works of two of the greatest rabbinic scholars of the nineteenth and twentieth centuries, the Chatam Sofer and Rabbi Moshe Feinstein, respectively.

The foundation of Judaism rests upon its ability to balance modernity with tradition, to faithfully maintain its adherence to the principles of the Written as well as the Oral Law, and above all to apply these principles to the context in which it finds itself. The people entrusted with this vital task are its rabbinic leadership. As aptly put by Rabbi Lord Jonathan Sacks, 'in ages of turbulence ... victory goes to the leader who can speak to the anxieties of the age'.[2] The purpose of this work is to seek to highlight some of the great rabbinic personalities who exemplified this trait. Through studying the variety of approaches adopted by them, together with the methodology they employed in doing so, it is hoped that new insights can be gained into Judaism's ability to respond to challenge.

To maintain continuity with Jewish tradition and heritage in the face of challenge is one of the central tasks of the Jewish people. *Challenge and Continuity* seeks to examine how this has been achieved by some of our greatest leaders, and thereby learn essential lessons for our future as a nation loyal to the Torah.

NOTES

1. Deuteronomy 17:8–11.
2. Jonathan Sacks, 'Fashioning the World Anew with Winged Thoughts', *The Times*, 21 November 2008.

Acknowledgements

This work would not have been possible without the support, guidance and encouragement of many people. In particular, I am deeply grateful to Chief Rabbi Ephraim Mirvis, Rabbi Lord Jonathan Sacks, Dayan Ivan Binstock, Professor Michael Berkowitz, Ilana Epstein, Rabbi Elchonon Feldman, Abi Kurzer, Michael Harris, Rabbi Michael Laitner, Rabbi Dr Naftali Lowenthal, Rabbi Daniel Roselaar, Professor Sacha Stern and Rabbi Dr Raphael Zarum. They have all graciously given of their time in a variety of ways to assist with this project, and I thank them all. My mother, Ruth Birnbaum, herself a published author, has been a wonderful source of inspiration and advice at all times. In addition, I thank the editor and staff at Vallentine Mitchell. Their superb dedication and professionalism has transformed this abstract idea into a reality.

I am also indebted to the Honorary Officers, Board of Management and members of the Hadley Wood Jewish Community, whose ongoing enthusiastic support for my scholarly endeavours has been nothing short of remarkable. I consider it a true privilege to serve as Rabbi of this unique and special community.

My father and uncle have kindly dedicated this book in memory of their late parents, and my grandparents, Sonia and Jack Birnbaum. In a world of free choice my grandparents chose to remain true to their heritage, and it is therefore entirely fitting that the dedication of this book belongs to them.

Finally, and most importantly of all, I thank my wonderful family for their unwavering support. To my children and especially my wife and partner in life, Elisheva, thank you for everything.

Yoni Birnbaum
5777 – 2017

PART I

Response to Modernity

1

Introduction

The onset of modernity in the late eighteenth and early nineteenth century brought with it particular challenges for contemporary rabbinic leadership. These challenges in turn both prompted and informed a myriad of responses on the part of successive generations of leading rabbis, many of whom were required to deal with issues that had never before undergone consideration. In understanding these responses, this section seeks to analyse and compare the responses of two of these leading *poskim*[1] (halakhic authorities), the Chatam Sofer (Rabbi Moshe Sofer, d. 1839, Hungary) and Rabbi Moshe Feinstein (d. 1986, USA), to the challenges of modernity, through an examination of their halakhic responsa.

Particular attention will be given in this context to the methodology used in these responsa and the fact that it often appears to be 'extra-halakhic' in nature, a term to be defined below. The central question is whether or not this was a new development, consequential to the new conditions of nineteenth to twentieth century modernity.

I will argue that this extra-halakhic approach does in fact have significant precedents in rabbinic literature. This will be demonstrated by analysing instances of parallel 'extra-halakhic' approaches found in the pre-modern literature. In turn this will provide an appropriate framework within which to assess the approaches of the Chatam Sofer and Rabbi Feinstein themselves.

The responsa literature has a long and varied history. However, as Menachem Elon observes,[2] whilst individual *responses* to particular halakhic questions posed are incorporated within the corpus of Talmudic and Midrashic literature,[3] dedicated works containing detailed individual responsa are not extant from this period. It is in the post-Talmudic period (post sixth century CE), therefore, that the first works devoted exclusively to responsa appear. Thus, it is only from the Geonic period (approximately 650–1050 CE) onwards that the responsa literature should correctly be treated as a separate genre of halakhic literature.[4] Hence, it is to the methodology adopted in this post-Talmudic genre of responsa, together with certain noteworthy references in the halakhic Codes, that we will be confining our initial study.

NOTES

1. A brief note on the use of italics and spelling of Hebrew words may be helpful. Italics will only be used for those words that are relatively uncommon. Other, more common, words, such as 'halakhic', will be treated as English language words and hence not italicized. In general, scholarly convention has been followed in terms of the spelling of Hebrew words, with the exception of the Hebrew letter '*het*', which has been written as 'ch' (as in the Scottish word 'loch'), rather than 'h'. Hence 'Chatam Sofer', rather than 'Hatam Sofer' and 'Shulchan Arukh', rather than 'Shulhan Arukh'. Other changes to scholarly spelling convention have also occasionally been made in order to ensure readability.
2. M. Elon, *Ha-Mishpat Ha-Ivri: Jewish Law: History Sources and Principles*, trans. B. Auerbach and M. Sykes (Philadelphia, PA: Jewish Publication Society, 1994), p.1455.
3. See for example *bGittin* 34b, regarding a written enquiry to Rabban Gamaliel asking for guidance in writing a bill of divorce where the husband's name was uncertain (cited in Elon, *Ha-Mishpat Ha-Ivri*, p.1454).
4. Ibid., p.1456.

2

A Question of Source

In outlining the fundamental importance of the responsa literature to the halakhic tradition in Judaism, Menachem Elon observes that central to understanding the methodology adopted by them is the fact that:

> Jewish law requires that no legal ruling be made except after a study of the various relevant opinions and approaches and after an examination of the correctness of each opinion in the light of the Talmudic sources ... these requirements have given rise to a cautious and sceptical attitude toward any ... that [is] not linked to the sources of the law.[1]

Thus, on a basic level, one would expect that a question posed in Jewish law would be resolved by reference to the paramount accepted Jewish *legal* texts, in other words, the *legalistic* sections of the Talmud. The resolution would then follow the subsequent application of these laws in the later halakhic codes, such as those authored by R. Yitzchak Alfasi (the 'Rif', d. 1103), R. Moshe ben Maimon ('Maimonides', d.1204), R. Asher b. Yechiel (the 'Rosh', d. 1328), R. Yaakov b. Asher (the 'Tur', d.1343) and later by the Shulchan Arukh, (R. Joseph Karo, d. 1575) and R. Moshe Isserlis (the 'Remah', d. 1572). It seems self-evident, therefore that it is to the legalistic portions of the Talmud that the halakhist should turn in order to work out what the 'practical halakhah' is. The aggadic sections of the Talmud, conversely, are of a very different nature, and, it would seem, should not be used as a source for the strict halakhic decision-making required of the writer. Indeed, support for this perspective can ostensibly be found in a statement in the Jerusalem Talmud, to the effect that, 'One does not learn (that is, render halakhic decisions) from the aggadah'.[2] The precise meaning of this important passage will be considered further below.

Defining the term 'aggadah', however, is not in and of itself straightforward. One reason for this is that in the process of Talmudic discourse, aggadic material is often interwoven with the halakhah. A story, for instance, may be introduced in order to prove a halakhic point, from which a tangential aggadic passage follows. Nevertheless, the provision of a working definition of 'aggadah' at this point is necessary in order to provide context for what follows.

The word 'aggadah' (or '*haggadah*' as it is sometimes called) is derived from the verb '*l'haggid*', meaning to relate or tell. Thus, many aggadic passages consist of stories of Talmudic Sages and their communities, which can often look somewhat simplistic to the untrained eye. Of crucial importance, however, is an appreciation of the opinions of later key rabbinic figures regarding the aggadic sections of the Talmud, treating them with the utmost respect and as concealing great mystical truths. To cite, for instance, a classic work on the aggadah authored by Rabbi Moshe Chaim Luzzatto (the 'Ramchal', d. 1746):

> ... therefore they (the Sages) decided to make a compromise. They would write down [these mystical ideas], in order that they would not be lost from succeeding generations, but in a hidden way and through the use of riddles.
>
> So that only one who has the keys, in other words, the principles through which [these] hints can be understood and these riddles explained, will be able to [properly] comprehend them. However, to one who has not received these keys they would remain before him like a sealed book, and as if they had not been written down at all.[3]

To Rabbi Luzzatto, therefore, the aggadah is sacred, its often apparent simplicity concealing deep mystical truths. In a similar vein, Maimonides expresses a deep sensitivity towards the aggadah, whilst simultaneously eschewing those who insist on always interpreting it in a literal sense. For him, the correct path is followed by those who:

> ...appreciate the greatness of the Sages ... and realise that their words have both a revealed and hidden meaning. Thus whenever they say something that appears extraordinary, they are speaking in a parable and riddle – for indeed this is the way of the greatest wise men.[4]

Nevertheless, expressing a belief in the mystical significance and depth of meaning behind the aggadic passages in the Talmud did not necessarily mean that these passages were viewed as appropriate material in terms of providing a *source* for the halakhah. Indeed, words of caution to this effect within the medieval rabbinic literature are relatively widespread. Thus, for instance, Rabbi Shmuel HaNaggid (d. 1056) in his *Introduction to the Talmud* writes: 'The *haggadah* is every explanation brought in the Talmud on any topic that is not [part of] a commandment ... and you should not learn from it[5] except for what appears reasonable.[6]

Similarly, the response of Nachmanides (R. Moshe ben Nachman, d. 1270) during the famous Disputation of Barcelona in 1263 to Christian citations of aggadic passages that appear to paint the Christian saviour in a negative manner, was simply to argue that since these passages are aggadic in nature, they are treated as non-binding, in a halakhic sense, by the Jewish people.[7] Whilst there are those who posit that Nachmanides argued thus in the course of the Disputation for political reasons, himself believing otherwise,[8] others such as Hyam Maccoby[9] have pointed to a degree of consistency between this and various other statements by Nachmanides in reference to aggadic passages throughout his writings, implying that this was indeed an accurate representation of his personally held opinion.[10]

In a later but important passage on the use of aggadah in the halakhic process, the well-known mishnaic commentator, Rabbi Yom Tov Lipmann Heller (author of the *Tosefot Yom Tov*,[11] d. 1660) states that:

> One cannot derive the halakhah from the Midrash Rabbot. For in the [Midrash] Rabbot, *Parshat Bereishit*, end of section 8, the Mishnah at the end of the sixth chapter of *Yevamot* is brought, wherein Rabbi Yochanan b. Nuri states that the commandment to be fruitful and multiply was said to both of them (i.e. Adam and Eve). And on this R. Jeremiah and R. Yitzhak b. Mirion in the name of R. Chaninah state that the halakhah is in accordance with him. Yet we do not rule this way! And so we have learnt in the Jerusalem Talmud (*Peah* chapter 2, cited above) ... [that] we do not learn from ... the aggadot.[12]

R. Heller in this passage appears to make an unequivocal statement regarding the halakhic status of the Midrash Rabbah and, by extension, the aggadah in general. Despite the fact that the midrash he refers to discusses a halakhic rather than aggadic passage regarding the obligation to procreate, and goes so far as to present a halakhic ruling about it, one 'cannot derive the halakhah' from it, due to its intrinsically 'non-halakhic' status.[13]

Nevertheless, despite these seemingly strict guidelines surrounding the halakhic process, certain modern scholars have argued that there has been a rejection of them in the modern period, and a move by halakhists towards a greater inclusion of 'non-legal' material (such as the aggadic sections of the Talmud) in the halakhic decision-making process. Thus, for example, in an article entitled 'The Emergence of Ultra-Orthodoxy: The Invention of a Tradition',[14] Michael Silber argued forcefully that:

> In general, while mainstream figures did not entirely ignore this extra-legal corpus, they did seek to minimize its impact on the *halakhic* process. The ultra-orthodox, on the other hand, adopted a diametrically opposite strategy ... wherever the body of legal traditions proper proved inadequate, their rule was to mobilise non-legal traditions to step into the halakhic breach.[15]

Silber's central thesis here rests on the fact that this was a *new* development in the process of halakhic decision-making. In his view, in order to respond to the challenges of both modern society and the Enlightenment, rabbinic scholars were forced to grant unprecedented *legal* weight to passages that were not previously utilized in such a manner. He identifies the Chatam Sofer as the one who began this process, later taken to an extreme by Akiva Yosef Schlesinger (b. Pressburg, 1821; d. Jerusalem 1922), whom Silber regards as 'the quintessence of the phenomenon (of ultra-orthodoxy)',[16] as demonstrated through his writings, advocating what Silber sees as an 'ultra-orthodox' approach to issues. Foremost amongst these is his polemical work, *Lev Ha'Ivri*,[17] a running commentary on the ethical will of the Chatam Sofer, first published in 1864 and later expanded in 1868. The central theme of this book is the obligation to 'battle' for the preservation of religious life in Judaism, in order to combat the 'threatening forces' of modernity.

In Silber's opinion, the key innovation of the Chatam Sofer and the subsequent rabbinic leaders who followed his path was that 'methods of casuistic, legal analysis were indiscriminately applied to [the] material'.[18] Thus, whereas previously these passages had been treated as non-literal, using, 'the mechanism which had guided Jews over the centuries in sifting, weighing, discarding and reconciling the multiplicity of aggadic statements',[19] they were now analysed in a very different light. Hence, according to Silber: 'If in fact there is reason to designate ultra-Orthodox Judaism "fundamentalist" it is precisely because of its tendency to ignore the "tradition" of these traditions in favour of a literal reading.'[20]

Analysis of Silber's comments in respect of Schlesinger himself is beyond the scope of this study. In a wider sense, however, the simplistic pattern and strict framework within which Silber characterizes the pre-Chatam Sofer halakhic process as confirming to is problematic, and it is this that is most relevant to this discussion.

Close examination of both the early responsa literature as well as the halakhic codes, such as those of Maimonides and the later Shulchan Arukh, reveal that the supporting literature utilized by a particular halakhic authority, or *posek*, in arriving at his halakhic conclusion will often be much broader than the legalistic sections of the Talmud themselves. Such 'extra-halakhic' material may indeed include, for instance, sources which are aggadic in nature. Alternatively, it may include considerations that appear devoid of any specific source at all, but are deemed necessary within the 'spirit of the law' and essential in order to achieve a particular aim, in relation to the challenges of the time, known collectively as *takkanot* (enactments).[21] It is this which provides an essential backdrop for an examination of the relatively modern responsa of the Chatam Sofer and R. Feinstein. In this context, we will also consider the very different conclusions to those of Silber reached by Elon in his *Ha'Mishpat Ha'Ivri* concerning the aggadah and the role it plays in the halakhic process.

In the first instance, it is quite clear that examples of the incorporation of 'extra-halakhic material' abound throughout the medieval rabbinic literature. For instance, Maimonides includes in his halakhic work a section entitled '*Hilkhot De'ot*' (Laws of Knowledge), codifying many ethical laws in what is clearly halakhic terminology. This, in turn, is followed by R. Joseph Karo in his Shulchan Arukh, who, following Maimonides, does similarly.[22]

In a more specific example from the beginning of the Shulchan Arukh,[23] a law is stated to the effect that it is forbidden for a Jewish male to walk a distance of four cubits with his head uncovered. However, the only sources for this appear to be aggadic in nature, as in this passage in the Tosefta: 'R. Huna the son of Joshua would not walk four cubits with his head uncovered. He would say "the Divine Presence is above my head"'.[24]

Clearly, in this instance, what is effectively a brief aggadic passage in the Talmud has entered the universally accepted corpus of Jewish law. Similarly, the numerous laws cited by R. Isserles[25] regarding the prayer to be recited by a mourner (the *Kaddish*) are based almost exclusively on an aggadic midrash.[26]

Thus, it is clear that aggadic sections of the Talmud have in fact been both utilized and referred to by post-Talmudic halakhists in their halakhic works when deemed appropriate. However, there is a need to examine whether this is also the case regarding the earlier responsa literature.

Of great importance in this connection is a work authored by R. Zvi Hirsch Chajes (d. 1855), entitled *Darkhei Horaah*.[27] In this work, R. Chajes devotes an entire section to an analysis of the aforementioned statement in the Jerusalem Talmud to the effect that 'one does not learn from the aggadah'.[28] The meaning of 'learn' in this context is in the sense of 'render legal decisions'. Thus, this statement would, at face value, appear to provide strong grounds for the argument that reliance upon aggadic passages in rendering halakhic decisions was, historically at least, deemed unacceptable.

However, R. Chajes proceeds to list numerous cases found in the responsa literature, from which it is evident that cases *were* in fact decided based upon the aggadah.[29] Several examples cited by him will be noted here. In responsum number 107 of R. Yaakov ben Asher (d. 1383), proof is adduced that a judge is permitted to decide a case on the basis of a high degree of probability, rather than absolutely proven fact. This is based upon the following passage in the Talmud:

> A certain man heard his wife say to her daughter, 'Why do you not observe more secrecy in your amours? I have ten children, and only one is from your father'. When [the man was] on his deathbed, he said, 'I leave all my property to one son'. They had no idea which of them he meant, so they consulted R. Bana'ah. He said to them: 'Go and knock at the grave of your father, until he gets up and tells you which one of you [he has made his heir]'. So they all went to do so. The one who was really his son, however, did not go. R. Bana'ah thereupon said: 'All the estate belongs to this one'.[30]

Hence, argues R. Chajes, what was ostensibly an aggadic, or at least semi-aggadic, passage in the Talmud became the primary source for a vitally important halakhic ruling, issued by one of the most senior medieval halakhists, concerning the judgment process in a Jewish court. Claiming that rabbinic authorities historically attempted to 'minimise the effect' of the aggadah on the halakhic process seems highly questionable in this light.

In a similar responsum, R. Shimon ben Zemach Duran (known as the Rashbez, d.1444)[31] also allowed judgment to be handed down based on probability, but in reliance upon an alternative aggadic passage,[32] wherein a Talmudic sage identified the thief of a silver cup based upon his misuse of the property of others in a different situation.

In yet another responsum,[33] R. David ben Solomon ibn Abi Zimra (known as the Radvaz, d.1573) held that a Jewish court was obligated to do whatever necessary in terms of judging the case, having no regard for a possible apostasy that could result from the losing party. In proving this, Radvaz cited the following passage:

> When Rabbi was dying he said: 'There is a [town called] Birtha di Satya in Babylon: today they have turned away from the Almighty – a fishpond overflowed on the Sabbath, and they went and caught the fish on the Sabbath', whereat R. Achi son of R. Josiah declared the ban [Heb. *cherem*] against them, and they renounced Judaism.[34]

Thus, basing himself on what was essentially an aggadic passage describing an event that occurred during Talmudic times, Radvaz issued a halakhic ruling, clearly intended to be binding upon his followers.

In another example, R. Chajes cites a ruling of R. Solomon ben Jechiel Luriah (known as the Maharshal, d.1574) in his work *Yam Shel Shelomoh* (first printed in 1616).[35] Basing himself upon an aggadic passage[36] describing the tragic death of the Talmudic sage R. Chaninah ben T'radion at the hands of the Romans, during which he refused to speed his own death in any way,[37] Maharshal ruled that even in a life-threatening situation, it was forbidden to cause harm to oneself.

A further fascinating example of the use of an aggadic passage in a halakhic context, albeit one not cited by R. Chajes, can be found in a responsum of Rashi (R. Solomon Yitzchaki, d.1105)[38] concerning the question of a marriage ceremony wherein both the couple involved and the required witnesses had previously been forcibly baptised. In dealing with the issue, Rashi argued that the woman concerned nevertheless required a *get* (bill of divorce), since we treat the marriage as halakhically valid. In support of his position, Rashi cited an aggadic passage in the Talmud[39] that elucidates a verse in the book of Joshua (chapter 7) concerning a man called Akhan, who was found to have illegally appropriated property from the conquered city of Jericho. The phrase used in the Bible on discovering his sin is '*chatah yisrael*' or 'Israel has sinned'. Thus, states the Talmud, we see that 'even though he had sinned, he was still called an Israelite', i.e. a member of the Jewish nation. Fascinatingly, Rashi utilized this passage, despite its aggadic nature, in order to provide a source for a halakhic ruling that the couple concerned should be treated as having had a valid Jewish marriage. This example is particularly noteworthy in the context of this discussion, as an aggadic passage was applied in order to solve a relatively 'new' problem that had arisen, namely the issue of forced conversions. In commenting on the significance of this application in particular, Katz notes that this responsum:

> ...has, since then, become a standard ruling in connexion with [the] definition of the status of the apostate. In its original Talmudic context this sentence appears in an aggadic setting only, and not in relation to apostasy. By using it in this striking manner, Rashi ensured the almost uncontested adoption of his definition.[40]

Thus, we once again see how the aggadah was in fact accepted as valid halakhic source material by central rabbinic figures of the medieval period in their responsa.

In light of these and other examples, R. Chajes argued that the statement of the Jerusalem Talmud that one 'may not learn from the aggadah' (cited above) did not refer to the aggadic passages in the Talmud at all.[41] Instead, he asserted that:

> ...this rule was not set out by the Sages of blessed memory because they treated the aggadic passages in a lighter manner. For, on the contrary, all their words are like fiery coals and we are obligated to accept them with reverence.[42]

He therefore postulated that it referred to specific situations, such as sermons that were delivered to the general public on the Sabbath and festivals, a significant proportion of which was devoted to 'aggadic' type material.[43] These, he argued, were never intended to be seen as a guide to the halakhah and were for ethical instruction purposes only. By contrast, general aggadic passages recorded in the Talmud are certainly valid as potential source material for halakhic rulings.[44]

Another interesting source in this context is the halakhic tradition validating the sale of *chametz* (leaven) on Passover. The Mishnah[45] states that it is permitted to have leaven in one's house on Passover belonging to a non-Jew. This is derived from a verse in Exodus: 'there shall be no leavened bread seen *with you*',[46] as opposed to that of a non-Jew which is permitted. There is, however, an additional source in the Tosefta which reads as follows:

> [In a situation where] an Israelite and a gentile were on a ship and there is *chametz* in the possession of the Israelite, he should sell it to the gentile, or give it to him as a present, and then re-purchase it from him after Passover. This is [allowed], however, only if he gives it to him as a complete [i.e. unconditional] gift.[47]

What is noteworthy about this example is the fact that until seventeenth-century Poland the application of this Tosefta was marginal. To be sure, Jews did sell their *chametz* to gentiles when necessary, but it was removed from the house for the duration of the festival. Thus, whilst this Tosefta is cited in the primary halakhic works of the late-medieval halakhists, it is generally recorded verbatim,[48] implying that its application may well have been treated as limited to the specific case discussed in the Tosefta. By the seventeenth-century, however, there were a large number of Jews working as innkeepers. They were involved in the production of grain-based alcohol in quantities too great to feasibly be removed over Passover. This prompted certain eminent halakhic authorities to utilize the remedy provided in the Tosefta, thereby allowing a formal sale to a non-Jew, even if the actual *chametz* remained within the domain of the Jew.

Reflecting this change in circumstances, R. Joel Sirkis (d.1640), a leading Polish rabbi, writes as follows in his commentary to the Tur:[49]

> In this country where the majority of business dealings are with alcohol, and it is impossible for them to sell to a non-Jew [to the extent that he takes it] outside the house ... there are grounds to permit one to sell all the leaven in the room to a non-Jew, and also the room itself he should sell to the non-Jew.[50]

Hence, although the Talmudic source here is not aggadic in nature, it provides a highly useful case study in how pre-Chatam Sofer halakhists could utilize what appears to be a relatively marginal Talmudic source in order to solve the halakhic problems of the day. Thus, once again, the characterisation of a straightforward direct application of halakhic principles set out in the codes of Jewish law in order to solve problems of the day is called into question.

As further support for this thesis, we will now consider Menachem Elon's conclusions regarding the significance of the aggadah in the context of the halakhic decision-making process. Elon argues that 'there is a persistent reciprocal relationship between halakhah and aggadah that finds expression in various ways'.[51] With reference to the sources mentioned above, amongst others, Elon demonstrates how one of the primary purposes of the aggadah is to provide a *philosophy* behind the halakhah. Indeed, it is only in this context that the fact that aggadic material could become the 'basis for normative rulings' can be understood.[52]

As evidence for this, Elon cites two responsa that are particularly noteworthy. One,[53] by R. Menachem Mendel Krochmal (Germany, d.1660),[54] was written in response to a suggestion by certain wealthy townspeople to grant a right to vote in town affairs only to those who had paid a substantial amount of tax, in other words, to the wealthy. In the responsum, R. Krochmal cites numerous aggadic passages that describe the efforts of the poor as equal to those of the rich,[55] thereby implying that a right to vote should not be determined on the basis of financial standing. Despite their homiletic style, writes Elon, R. Krochmal sees in them the all-important philosophy *behind* the halakhah – and it is this that allows him to adduce them as support for a legal ruling.

In the second example cited by Elon,[56] the respondent, R. Shimon b. Zemach Duran,[57] was asked to rule on whether a will that left money to a synagogue at the expense of a needy legal heir, although (according to the questioner) halakhically valid, should at least be considered 'morally deficient'.[58] In what Elon terms an 'unprecedented ruling', R. Duran ruled that the will was halakhically void altogether, and that the needy relative *would* in fact inherit the estate. Despite the apparent existence of halakhic sources that validate a will such as this, R. Duran relied in his ruling upon an aggadic passage in the Jerusalem Talmud,[59] in which Rav commented on how wrong it was to spend money on building a synagogue at the expense of helping poor people. On this basis, R. Duran ruled that the objective of the will itself was a transgression, and hence invalid altogether.

Thus, in this instance an aggadic source superseded the implication of the primary halakhic source, due to the particular circumstances of the case. Elon observes that the implications of this responsum are 'extremely far-reaching'. Admittedly with a degree of 'judicial courage and statesmanship', R. Duran deduced a principle from an aggadic passage in order to overrule a previously 'settled legal ruling'. The key implication of this, comments Elon, is that: 'the halakhah and aggadah each provide resources for the other. It is an illustration of the practice of the halakhic authorities to base their decisions, when reason and justice require, on the philosophy of the halakhah, which was heavily coloured by the aggadah.'[60]

The importance of Elon's analysis in the context of our discussion is clear, and will be returned to in more detail below. At present, one further point will be noted. To Elon, the rationale behind utilizing the aggadah in this way, aside from its place as an integral part of the Oral Law, is the fact that:

> Reaching legal decisions on the basis of the principles and concepts taken from the world of the aggadah is, in the final analysis, decision-making on the basis of the legal reasoning of the halakhic authorities, which ... is one of the legal sources of Jewish law.[61]

This conception of the importance of the process of 'legal reasoning' to the halakhic decision maker, or *posek,* is central to an understanding of the methodology of both the Chatam Sofer and R. Feinstein, as will be discussed further below.

There are a further set of sources that are appropriate to adduce at this point, in reference to the use of extra-halakhic considerations when issuing a halakhic ruling. These sources relate to the question of whether it is appropriate for a *posek* to take into account the *consequences* that a particular ruling may have, rather than issuing a decision on strict halakhic grounds alone. In Talmudic terminology, this is sometimes referred to as '*le-migdar miltha*' (lit. to fence around the matter).[62]

According to the simple model of a halakhic process determined on the basis of legal precedent alone (as suggested by Silber), this is surprising. If according to the strict letter of the law something is allowed, so it should remain, regardless of the consequences the ruling could have. As evidence of Silber's approach to this issue, it is worth referring to his critique[63] of Hillel Lichtenstein's[64] reply to a (halakhically justifiable) argument allowing the brewing of alcohol on the Sabbath through the agency of a non-Jew.[65] Lichtenstein's scathing response was to quote the Chatam Sofer as having taught of the importance of the 'fifth volume of the Shulchan Arukh', namely 'to rule and teach in accordance with the state of the generation'. Thus, continued Lichtenstein, even if a 'voice from Heaven' would issue forth permitting the brewing on the Sabbath, I would say 'this is not in Heaven (i.e. we are not obliged to listen)!'[66] Hence, argues Silber:

> ...even the Shulchan Arukh could not be accepted as the final arbiter. The decisive authority *for the ultra-Orthodox* mine resided

> not in the letter of the law (even as recorded in the Shulchan Arukh) but in its spirit.[67]

As in the case of the argument presented above regarding the use of the aggadah as source material, the central claim here is not that Silber is incorrect in asserting that during and after the nineteenth century halakhic authorities took into account the spirit of the law and a concern for the consequences of their decisions in issuing rulings, for they evidently did do so. Instead, it is with his implicit argument that there is a lack of historical precedent in the responsa literature for this (in that it was an invention of the 'extreme' ultra-Orthodox of the nineteenth century) that we take issue. Hence, three historical examples will now be cited from the corpus of the earlier responsa literature in which this approach clearly *was* adopted.

The first of these examples is found in the responsa of R. Meir ben Yekutiel of Rothenburg (d.1298),[68] author of the *Haggahot Maimoniot*, a series of glosses on Maimonides' Mishnah Torah. Especially noteworthy about this work is the collection of responsa appended to it, designed to present the views of several Ashkenazic scholars, in contrast to those of Maimonides himself. In responsum number 11 of this collection, the author discusses the case of a woman whose husband fell into a body of water without visible boundaries. As stated in the Talmud,[69] it is forbidden for her to remarry, due to a concern that the first husband may still be alive In this situation, she is referred to as an *agunah*, or 'chained woman'. The question arises, however, as to what the law would be when she wilfully ignored this prohibition (as opposed to a situation in which she was granted a rabbinical permit) and did in fact remarry. Should she be forced to leave the second husband?

In responding to this question, R. Meir notes that common opinion seems to be that she should be allowed to remain with him, on the basis that the Talmud does not explicitly rule otherwise, and indeed, in a variant situation in the same passage,[70] allows her to remain with her husband *post facto*. However, R. Meir forcefully disagrees with this on two grounds. Firstly, if this was to be permitted, every woman in this unfortunate situation would follow suit, as once married she would effectively have achieved a *fait accompli*. Furthermore:

> If so [that once married she could remain thus] we would make the rabbinical decree [against remarrying] into a mockery – for we would effectively let everyone destroy the fence erected by our Sages without saying anything to them at all![71]

This is therefore an early example of a halakhic responsum which takes careful consideration of the consequences that a particular ruling would be likely to have, and allows this to serve as a primary consideration in the decision-making process – effectively outlawing something not explicitly prohibited in theTalmud itself. This calls into question the assumption that to issue a ruling on such grounds is a relatively recent phenomenon.

In a second example of this approach, a ruling is given in a responsum authored by R. Levi ibn Habib (d.1545)[72] not to teach certain Kabbalistic doctrines in public. This was not because of any particular law against doing so, but due to a concern that those who are not accustomed to such doctrines may consider them so strange as to bring Judaism in general into disrepute. In this case too, the halakhic ruling clearly took into account the fact that it could lead to certain undesirable consequences.

The final example we will cite is found in the responsa of R. Moshe Isserlis.[73] The question concerned a possible *mamzer* (literally 'bastard', referring to a child of an adulterous or incestuous union) who wished to serve as a religious judge or *dayyan*. In this particular scenario, the person in question was halakhically considered a '*shetuki*', meaning one whose mother is identifiable but not his father, hence treated as a 'doubtful *mamzer*'.[74] In the responsum[75] R. Isserlis stated categorically that according to the strict letter of the law there would seem to be no prohibition against him occupying such a position. Nevertheless, quoting other senior rabbinical figures, he concluded as follows:

> All this I have spoken according to [how] the halakhah [is], but not in terms of practical application in the case under discussion ... [for] they decided not to elevate him [to the position]. Not due to the strict letter of the law, but since it would be a disgrace to the Torah, for people would treat him disrespectfully.[76]

Hence, once again, we see that extra-halakhic considerations played an important role, historically, in the halakhic decision-making process. It is also noteworthy that Elon in his discussion of the Talmudic principle of '*le-migdar miltha*' ('fence around the matter') stresses the fact that, historically, certain enactments that fall under this category, such as those concerning the *agunah* (as above) are:

> ...among the most far-reaching exercises of the legislative prerogative of the halakhic authorities, have become permanent

> parts of Jewish law, and hundreds of their provisions and rules constitute an essential part of Jewish family law.[77]

These sources, together with the earlier ones cited above regarding the use and application of aggadic passages in the context of the halakhah, provide the necessary historical background to accurately examine the methodology of the Chatam Sofer and R. Feinstein in their response to modernity.

NOTES

1. Menachem Elon, *Ha-Mishpat Ha-Ivri: Jewish Law: History Sources and Principles,* trans. Bernard Auerbach and Melvin Sykes (Philadelphia, PA: Jewish Publication Society, 1994), p.1463.
2. *yPe'ah* 2:4 and in similar terminology in *yChagigah* 1:8.
3. R. Moses Hayyim Luzzatto, *Maamar Al Hahaggadot* (Essay on the Aggadah) (Warsaw: Ahavah Publications, 1936), p.2.
4. *Commentary on the Mishnah*, Trac. Sanhedrin (Jerusalem: Mossad HaRav Kook, 1963–67), Introduction to Chapter 8.
5. That is, in a halakhic sense.
6. R. Samuel HaNagid, *Introduction to the Talmud* (Jerusalem: Talman Publishers, 1981 [First published Istanbul, 1510]). Subsequently incorporated as part of Tractate Berachot in the Vilna edition of the Talmud.
7. Cited in H. Maccoby, *Judaism on Trial: Jewish-Christian Disputations in the Middle Ages* (London: Littman Library of Jewish Civilisation, 1993), p.67 et al.
8. See for instance Y. Baer, 'L'bikoret havikhuhim shel rabi Yehiel MiParis v'rabi Moshe ben Nahman'(Heb), *Tarbiz*, 2, no.2 (1931), pp.172–87.
9. Maccoby, *Judaism on Trial*, loc. cit. On Nachmanides' approach to aggadah in general see further Jonathan Sacks, *One People?* (London: Littman Library of Jewish Civilisation, 1993), pp.93–4.
10. For extensive treatment of this topic see further Maccoby, *Judaism on Trial*. Regarding methods employed by Jewish leaders in disputations with Christians more generally see Jacob Katz, *Exclusiveness and Tolerance* (Oxford: Oxford University Press, 1961), pp.106–13.
11. R. Yom Tov Heller, *Tosefot Yom Tov* (Jerusalem: Horev Publishing House, 1993 [First published Cracow, 1543]).
12. Commentary to *mBerakhot* 5:4.
13. It is, however, important to note that R. Heller's words could also conceivably be construed as a polemical statement regarding the reliability (in a halakhic context) of the relatively recently published *Midrash Rabbah to the Five Books of the Torah* (Venice, 1545). This work was in fact a compilation of at least ten different midrashim (see the *Jewish Encyclopaedia* (New York: Funk and Wagnalls, 1906), entry on '*Midrash Haggadah*'). Further elaboration on this issue is beyond the scope of this study.
14. Michael Silber, 'The Emergence of Ultra-Orthodoxy – The Invention of a Tradition', in Jack Wertheimer (ed.), *The Uses of Tradition* (New York: Jewish Theological Seminary of America, 1992), pp.23–84.
15. Ibid., p.60.
16. Ibid., p.37. For further discussion regarding Schlesinger's life and literary career, see Michael Silber, 'Alliance of the Hebrews, 1863–1875: The diaspora roots of an

ultra-Orthodox proto-Zionist utopia in Palestine', *Journal of Israeli History: Politics, Society, Culture*, 27, no.2 (2008), pp.119–47.

17. Akiva Yoseph Schlesinger, *Lev Ha'Ivri* (Lemberg: Goldberg, 1873).
18. Silber, 'The Emergence of Ultra-Orthodoxy', p.60.
19. Ibid., p.61.
20. Ibid.
21. For a detailed overview and discussion of the history and process of *takkanot*, see Elon, *Ha'Mishpat Ha'Ivri*, Vol.2, pp.546–621.
22. See, for example, *Shulchan Arukh*, Orach Chayyim, sec. 170.
23. Orach Chayyim 2:4.
24. *tKidd.* 31a.
25. *Shulchan Arukh*. Yoreh Deah 376:5.
26. Kallah Rabbata 2.
27. Rabbi Zvi Hersh Chajes, *Darkhei Horaah* (Zolkiew: Meyerhoffer, 1842).
28. *yPe'ah* 2:4.
29. Chajes, *Darkhei Horaah*, section 2, p.12.
30. *bBaba Bathra* 58a. Trans. Isidore Epstein (ed.), *The Soncino Talmud* (London: Soncino Press, 1948).
31. Rabbi Shimon ben Zemach Duran, *Sheilot U'Teshuvot Tashbetz* (Jerusalem: Machon Yerushalayim, 1998 [First published Amsterdam: 1738]), vol.3, section 168.
32. *b.Baba Metziah* 24a.
33. R. David Ibn Abi Zimra, *Sh'eilot U'Teshuvot Radvaz* (Jerusalem: Walden, 1972 [First published Venice: 1749]), vol.1, section 187.
34. *bKidd.* 71a. Trans. Epstein, *The Soncino Talmud.*
35. *Baba Kammah* 88:58.
36. *b'Aboda Zara* 18a.
37. The text of the Talmud reads: ''Open then thy mouth' [said they] 'so that the fire enter into thee.' He replied, 'Let Him who gave me [my soul] take it away, but no one should injure oneself.'' (trans. Epstein, ibid).
38. *Teshuvot Rashi* (New York: Israel Elfenbein, 1943), sec. 171. The historic significance of this particular responsum is discussed at length in Jacob Katz, 'Though he sinned, he remains an Israelite' (Heb.), *Tarbiz*, 27, no.2/3 (1957–58), pp.203–17.
39. *bSan.* 44a.
40. Katz, *Exclusiveness and Tolerance*, p.70.
41. Chajes, *Darkhei Horaah*, p.13.
42. Ibid.
43. As evidence of this practice in Talmudic times, he cites a passage in *bShab.* 30a, in which a question of halakhah was asked, and the answer prefaced with words of ethical instruction related to the subject matter of the question.
44. For further references and support for this interpretation, see Elon, *Ha'Mishpat Ha'Ivri*, Vol.1, p.95.
45. *Pesachim* 2:1.
46. Exodus 12:20.
47. *tPes.* 2:12.
48. Thus, for example, Maimonides writes: 'A Jew and a gentile are traveling together in a ship, and the Jew possesses *chametz.* When the fifth hour [on the fourteenth of Nisan] arrives – behold, he should sell it to the gentile or give it to him as a present. He may return and buy it back from him after Pesach, as long as he gives it to him as an outright present.' (Laws of Chametz and Matzah in *Mishneh Torah*, trans. Eliyahu Touger (New York: Moznaim Publishers, 1997) , 4:6).

49. Halakhic codification written by R. Jacob ben Asher (known as the *Ba'al HaTurim* after his work on the Torah), d.1340.
50. Commentary of R. Joel Sirkis, *Bayyit Chadash (BaCH)* (Jerusalem: Machon Yerushalayim, 1993–94 [First published Cracow: 1631–39]), Orach Chayyim section 448.
51. Elon, *Ha'Mishpat Ha'Ivri*, Vol.1, p.94.
52. Ibid., p.95.
53. Cited in ibid., pp.96–9.
54. R. Menahem Mendel ben R. Abraham Krochmal, *Responsa Zemach Zedek* (Jerusalem: Wagshal, 1982 [First published Altdorf: 1775]), no.2.
55. As in *bMenachot* 110a referring to the equal acceptability in the eyes of G-d of the humble bird offering of a poor man.
56. Elon, *Ha'Mishpat Ha'Ivri*, Vol.1, 99–102.
57. Duran, *Sheilot U'Teshuvot Tashbetz*, Vol.3, no.190.
58. As noted by Elon (loc.cit.), according to Jewish law, a will is valid as long as it is properly executed, however disinheriting one's heirs is considered to be something that the Sages are 'displeased with' (cf. *bBaba Bathra* 133b).
59. *yPe'ah* 8:9.
60. Elon, *Ha'Mishpat Ha'Ivri*, Vol.1, p.102.
61. Ibid. p.104.
62. In this connection, see Elon's analysis of the application of this principle in ibid., Vol.1, pp.533–6. In identifying the Talmudic source for this concept he cites (p.533) *bYev*. 90b, in reference to the incident (I Kings 21) of Elijah offering sacrifices on Mt Carmel (despite the existence at the time of a prohibition against doing so outside the Temple) in order to disprove the idolatrous prophets of Ba'al. It is in justifying his actions (as essential to safeguard the future of the Jewish people) that the Talmud applies this phrase.
63. Silber, 'The Emergence of Ultra-Orthodoxy', p.50.
64. Died 1891, father in law of Schlesinger and co-author of the *Pesaq Din of Michalowce* of November 1865 (see below).
65. Silber, 'The Emergence of Ultra-Orthodoxy', suggests that the reference is to a proposed bill of sale drawn up by R. Chaim Halberstam of Sanz in the late 1850s.
66. Cf. *bBaba Metzia* 59b.
67. Silber, 'The Emergence of Ultra-Orthodoxy', p.50. See also Jacob Katz, *The Shabbes Goy: A Study in Halakhic Flexibility* (Philadelphia, PA: Jewish Publication Society, 1989), pp.204–15.
68. R. Meir ben Yekutiel, *Haggahot Maimoniot L'Sefer Nashim* (Jerusalem: Hotzaat Shabse Frankel, 1972).
69. *bYev.* 121a.
70. *bYev.* 121b.
71. Yekutiel, *Haggahot Maimoniot*, p.429.
72. R. Levi ibn Habib, *Sh'eilot U'teshuvot* (Venice: 1565), Nos.8 and 75.
73. R. Moses Isserlis, *Teshuvot Remah* (Jerusalem: Siev, 1971).
74. Cf. *bKidd.* 73a.
75. Isserlis, *Teshuvot Remah*, no.24.
76. Ibid., para. 5.
77. Elon, *Ha'Mishpat Ha'Ivri*, p.534.

3

Two Great Rabbinic Leaders: A Historical Overview

Moses Sofer was born in Frankfurt in 1762 and studied there in his youth under the tutelage of R. Pinchas Horowitz (Chief Rabbi of Frankfurt, d.1805) and R. Nathan Adler (d.1800). At the age of 19, Sofer followed his teacher R. Adler in his departure from Frankfurt due to the rabbinical opposition there towards his mystical leanings and ostensibly innovative path. Sofer himself gradually grew in stature, due in no small part to his exceptional scholarship and moral character, serving first as Rabbi of Dresnitz in Moravia, then of Mattersdorf, and finally in 1806 as Rabbi of Pressburg, Bratislava; a position he would occupy until his passing in 1839.

When his first wife died childless in 1812, he married the daughter of the well-known Talmudic scholar, R. Akiva Eger (Rabbi of Posen, d.1873), and their children formed the basis of the Sofer rabbinic dynasty, the influence of which spread far beyond Pressburg itself. His son Shimon later became Rabbi of Cracow and his son-in-law Solomon Zalman Spitzer served as Rabbi of the Orthodox community of Vienna.

Although very few of his writings were published during his lifetime, following his death his halakhic responsa were published in seven volumes as *Sh'eilot U'Teshuvot Chatam Sofer* (1855–1912),[1] after the title of which he came to be known, as well as his commentaries on the Talmud[2] and the Torah.[3]

Of utmost importance, however, to understanding the historical significance of the Chatam Sofer in particular, is an appreciation of the social context within which he lived. Jacob Katz[4] identifies the two major modern liberalistic influences on European Jewry that the Chatam Sofer sought to both restrict and combat throughout his ministry as that of the *maskilim* (Jewish Enlightenment) and the nascent Reform movement. In Katz's view, the Chatam Sofer sought to combat these influences through a combination of both the force of his personality together with the recourse of turning to the government for assistance whenever possible.[5]

As an example, Katz cites a memorandum of the Chatam Sofer dated 25 October 1832, in which he requests that both rabbis and local Jewish community officials be allowed to enlist the assistance of local authorities in the enforcement of the observance of religious laws.[6]

However, as Silber correctly notes, in the context of his response to these liberal trends it was through his written works that the Chatam Sofer ultimately left his greatest legacy. Silber's own central thesis in this connection, one which will be examined further below, is that the Chatam Sofer had:

> ...propounded an ideology which sought to provide a new rationale for besieged traditional values and institutions. In a studied antithesis of the Jewish Enlightenment and Reform Judaism, he had argued the merits of the traditional educational curriculum against that of the Haskalah; of exile and alienation against emancipation and integration ... of tradition against reason.[7]

A similar perspective on the Chatam Sofer's approach is adopted by Adam Ferziger. In describing his methodology in combating reform, Ferziger writes:

> When confronted by changes in the normative religious behaviour of his contemporaries, as well as by Reform ideological ferment, he attempted to place stumbling blocks against further desertion. By endorsing a policy of redefining that which had until then been considered a custom as a full-fledged prohibition,[8] he aimed to ensure that those who remained observant would treat all aspects of tradition with an equal degree of gravity.[9]

Thus, in the opinion of both Silber and Ferziger, the Chatam Sofer's uncompromising stance in the defence of 'tradition' against the products of modernity, paradoxically necessitated a departure from tradition in terms of the particular methodology he adopted.[10] Whether indeed they are correct in asserting that in doing so the Chatam Sofer had sought to provide a 'new rationale' for traditional Judaism will be considered in detail below.

We will now provide a brief historical overview and social context for Rabbi Moshe Feinstein.

Moshe Feinstein was born in 1895 in Uzda, Belarus, a city near Minsk, where his father served as rabbi. Following his studies in yeshivah, he was appointed rabbi of the Belarussian town of Luban, a position he held for sixteen years, until Soviet oppression forced him and his family to emigrate to the United States in 1936.

After his relocation, he settled in New York's Lower East Side and became the dean of a *yeshivah*, Mesivtha Tifereth Jerusalem, later establishing another branch of the institution in Staten Island. Throughout the next fifty years, until his passing in 1986, R. Feinstein became especially renowned as a *posek*, or halakhic adjudicator, answering halakhic queries from all over the Jewish world.

In contrast to the Chatam Sofer whose works were only published posthumously, it was specifically through the publication of R. Feinstein's writings, beginning with the first volume of his *Iggrot Moshe* in 1959,[11] that his rulings entered the public domain and took on an authoritative status, becoming a widely-accepted source of legal precedent in Jewish law. Seven volumes of this work appeared during his lifetime (1959–1985), with a further two volumes published posthumously, in 1996 and 2011. His other important works include *Dibrot Moshe*,[12] consisting of novellae on the Talmud, and *Darash Moshe*,[13] a commentary on the Torah.

In a degree of similarity with the Chatam Sofer, however, the importance of the social context within which R. Feinstein issued his halakhic rulings cannot be overstated. Living in post-war twentieth century America, he was called upon to answer questions on such diverse topics as artificial insemination, brain-stem death, women's rights, contemporary business ethics, vivisection, genetic illnesses, cosmetic surgery, synagogue practice and the status of civil marriage, to name but a few. Furthermore, many of these topics, due to their nature, had never previously been considered from a perspective of Jewish law. Hence, R. Feinstein's responsa provide fascinating material for a study on the methodology of the responsa literature in general, as well as the use of 'extra-legal' sources in particular.

Of equal importance in this connection is the existence and prominence of the American non-Orthodox movements at the time that Rabbi Feinstein issued his rulings, and in particular the Reform and Conservative movements. R. Feinstein was consistently called upon, in a not dissimilar way to the Chatam Sofer, to provide an Orthodox response to the innovations in Jewish law advocated by these institutions. In his own lifetime he thereby earned a reputation as:

> ...the leading Orthodox halakhic authority in the United States ... because of his willingness to deal with the problems facing observant Jews living in the radically changed world of modernity ... His responsa are the most widely cited of any modern authority.[14]

In the course of doing so, his works achieved great significance, not only in terms of their final halakhic rulings, but also in terms of the *methodology* they adopted in order to reach these conclusions. Hence they merit detailed study.

NOTES

1. R. Moses Sofer, *Sheilot U'Teshuvot Chatam Sofer* (Jerusalem: Machon L'Hotza'at Sefarim V'Cheker Kitvei Yad Al Shem HaHatam Sofer, 2008 [First published Pressburg, Bratislava: Anton Schmidt Printing Press, 1859]).
2. R. Moses Sofer, *Chiddushei Chatam Sofer* (Mihalevitz: Greenfeld Publishing, 1928).
3. R. Moses Sofer, *Chatam Sofer Al Chamisha Chumshei Torah* (Mihalevitz: Greenfeld Publishing, 1928).
4. Jacob Katz, *A House Divided* (Hanover, NH: Brandeis University Press, 1998), p.34.
5. Ibid.
6. Ibid., p.283, citing L. Low, *Zur Neureren Geschichte der Juden in Ungarn* (Budapest: 1874), pp.153–5.
7. Michael Silber, 'The Emergence of Ultra-Orthodoxy – The Invention of a Tradition', in Jack Wertheimer (ed.), *The Uses of Tradition* (New York: Jewish Theological Seminary of America, 1992), p.29.
8. For further discussion on the Chatam Sofer's use of the Talmudic phrase '"new things" are forbidden from the Torah in all situations' (*mOrlah* 3:9), to which Ferziger makes reference to here, see below.
9. Adam S. Ferziger, 'Religious Zealotry and Religious Law: Rethinking Conflict and Coexistence', *The Journal of Religion*, 84 (January 2004), p.50.
10. Silber, 'The Emergence of Ultra-Orthodoxy', 26. Essentially the same point is made by Ferziger (loc. cit.), who refers to 'the relative ease with which those rabbis who opposed modernity have been willing to redefine certain halakhic principles in order to achieve their goals'.
11. R. Moshe Feinstein, *Igrot Moshe* (New York: privately published, 1959–2011).
12. R. Moshe Feinstein, *Dibrot Moshe* (Bnei Brak: 1983).
13. R. Moshe Feinstein, *Darash Moshe* (New York: Mesorah Publications, 1994), published posthumously.
14. David Novak, 'Modern Responsa: 1800 to the Present', in N.S. Hecht, B.S. Jackson, S.M. Passamaneck, D. Piattelli and A.M. Rabello (eds), *An Introduction to the History and Sources of Jewish Law* (New York: Oxford University Press, 1996), p.394.

4

Responding to Modernity

The following chapter focuses on a detailed examination of the methodology adopted by the Chatam Sofer and R. Feinstein in the context of modernity, in light of the historical analysis presented in Chapter 2.

In March 1830, a rabbi asked the Chatam Sofer whether it would be permissible to acquiesce to the request of his community to relocate the *bimah* (desk upon which the Torah reading takes place) from the middle of the synagogue to the front, for aesthetic purposes.[1] In his response, ruling against allowing the change, the Chatam Sofer cited two Talmudic passages that are of particular interest in the context of this discussion.

The first of these reads as follows:

> It has been taught: R. Judah stated, 'He who has not seen the double colonnade of Alexandria in Egypt has never seen the glory of Israel ... it sometimes held twice the number of people that went forth from Egypt ... and a *wooden platform in the middle* upon which the attendant of the Synagogue stood with a scarf in his hand. When the time came to answer 'Amen', he waved his scarf and all the congregation duly responded'.[2] [Italics mine]

This passage, wrote the Chatam Sofer, is the source for necessitating the placement of the *bimah* in the middle of the synagogue. Importantly, at no point did the Chatam Sofer appear disturbed by the fact that this ostensibly aggadic passage could provide a source for his halakhic ruling. Moreover, its reference to the 'platform' being in the 'middle' of the synagogue in Alexandria could be taken as merely incidental to the issue under discussion in the Talmud. Yet, for the

Chatam Sofer, it is clear that this in no way detracted from his admission of it as valid source material.

This particular ruling of the Chatam Sofer was also particularly surprising for another reason, and it was this that prompted him to cite a second supporting Talmudic passage.[3] In the commentary to Maimonides written by the author of the Shulchan Arukh, R. Joseph Karo, a ruling was specifically given to the effect that:

> ...placement [of the *bimah*] in the centre is not mandatory; everything depends on the time and the place ... in our time when unfortunately our synagogues are small and everyone can hear well,[4] it is more pleasing that it be to one side rather than in the middle.[5]

It was this earlier lenient ruling that appeared to necessitate the justification by the Chatam Sofer of his contrastingly strict application of the aggadic passage concerning the synagogue in Alexandria mentioned previously. More fundamentally, the second Talmudic passage quoted by the Chatam Sofer in order to further substantiate his argument is of vital importance in understanding a key aspect of his general halakhic philosophy. At the end of his response to the questioner, he quoted the following Mishnah: 'the new produce is prohibited by the Torah in all places'.[6]

This law refers to the yearly new crop, known as *chadash*. The Mishnah cited states that the new crop is Biblically prohibited to be consumed until a special offering, known as the '*omer*', was brought in the Temple, or until the date of the 16th of the month of Nissan in the Temple's absence. However, the Chatam Sofer utilized this Mishnaic phrase as a type of slogan to indicate his general approach towards innovations that represented a break with past tradition.[7] Thus, in the context of this responsum regarding the re-location of the *bimah,* the Chatam Sofer refered to this passage in order to stress the importance of the issue:

> ...the principle is that 'new things' are forbidden from the Torah in all situations ... and ... [he will be] remembered for good [in] objecting forcefully in order to ensure that the 'holy place' is in the correct location.[8]

Aside from the fact that the location of the *bimah* in the centre does indeed have a source in Talmudic literature, it was especially important for the Chatam Sofer not to allow its re-location due to the fact that this could lead to severe *consequences*, and in particular a strengthening of the early Reform groups that sought to follow the Christian style of locating the altar at the front of the Church. In this manner, the Chatam Sofer justified the stricter approach that he took in this instance to that of earlier authorities. For in the much earlier time of R. Joseph Karo, such considerations were not relevant.

Thus, both policy and a consideration of the social implications that his rulings would have were clearly of importance to the Chatam Sofer in his decision-making process. As an aside, it is noteworthy that in this particular case, the Chatam Sofer's ruling was to indeed have far-reaching consequences. Included in the famous *Pesak Din of Michalowce* of November 1865,[9] largely on the basis of this responsum, was a specific prohibition against building a synagogue with a *bimah* that was not in the centre, to the extent that even entering such a synagogue was 'banned'.

This initial example of a responsum by the Chatam Sofer provides us with a valuable insight into his general methodology in responding to questions of this type. One can discern a combination of factors that guide him in reaching a decision. In the first place, he identifies a Talmudic source for the ruling and, importantly, allows an aggadic passage to be relied upon for this purpose, something we have provided ample precedent for in the earlier responsa literature, as detailed above. His usage of the aggadah appears to fit Elon's evaluation of the central role it plays as providing a, 'resource for the halakhah where necessary'.[10] But, crucially, the strength and import given to the ruling also stems from a careful appreciation of the *consequences* it will have and the social context within which it is designed to operate. This, too, is a factor that we have identified clear precedent for in the earlier responsa literature. Its application, however, merits further discussion and will be considered in more detail below.

Rabbi Feinstein was posed a similar question regarding the location of the *bimah* by a rabbi living in Kansas in 1959.[11] In his response, however, he approached the issue in a markedly different manner, respectfully noting the response of the Chatam Sofer, yet qualifying it:

> Certainly the *bimah* should be constructed in the centre. However, concerning praying in a synagogue where it has not been built in the middle, I see no prohibition.[12]
>
> And [concerning] that which it is reported that in Hungary this was [indeed] forbidden, the accuracy of this [report] is not known with certainty, and it is logical [to assume] that this was only in those places where this was enacted due to the [influence of]

> Reform. For in those places, this [innovation signified] the beginnings of the ... Reform movement.
>
> But in other places where their intention was not due to Reform [influences], but simply in order that there should be more seats [available] ... one should not prohibit [a person] from praying there. For this is not one of the primary rules of the synagogue, rather simply in order that everyone should be able to hear the Torah reading.

Evidently, R. Feinstein did not challenge the ruling of the Chatam Sofer on the grounds that his source was only based upon an aggadic passage. Instead, he argued that the *strength* of the prohibition in this case depended upon the social circumstances at the time of its enactment. Thus, although for the Chatam Sofer and successive generations in Hungary this ruling may have been deemed crucial to uphold at all costs in the Orthodox 'battle' against the nascent Reform movement, such would not necessarily be the case in twentieth-century America. Perhaps we can speculate that by then this was no longer one of the defining issues distinguishing Orthodoxy from Reform. Indeed, elsewhere in his responsa, R. Feinstein himself demonstrated vigorous opposition to other non-Orthodox innovations, an issue discussed in more detail below.

Hence, we can tentatively conclude that the *variable* in the approach taken by the Chatam Sofer and R. Feinstein in responding to this particular question is a result of the second of the two factors noted above, namely, '*le-migdar milta*'.[13] The potential source for a requirement to place the *bimah* in the center is agreed upon. The *extent*, however, to which account must be taken of the consequences that the ruling may have (and hence the strength with which it is to be enforced) is by definition, variable. It depends upon the social context and climate within which the responsum was issued, and the highly attuned awareness and sensitivity of the halakhic authority in question to that environment.

Further support for this can be adduced from an additional example of a similar difference in approach between the Chatam Sofer and R. Feinstein in a different context. The issue under discussion concerned the question of whether it was permitted for a man to shave his beard on *Chol Hamoed*, the intermediate days of the festivals of Passover and Sukkoth.

As background, the Talmud[14] prohibits the shaving of the beard on these days, due to a concern that if this were permitted there would be a tendency to leave doing so until then (when work pressures are reduced due to the holiday), thus leading to the inevitable consequence of entering the first part of the festival looking unkempt. One late medieval authority, however, Rabbi Jacob b. Meir (known as Rabbeinu Tam, d.1171), is quoted as having permitted the shaving of the beard on *Chol Hamoed* as long as it was in fact shaved on the eve of the festival as well. On this basis, in extenuating circumstances and with particular riders, R. Ezekiel b. Judah Landau of Prague (known as the Nodah Bi'Yehudah, d.1793) had permitted one who had shaved on the eve of the festival to also do so on *Chol Hamoed.*[15] It was with this permissive ruling that the Chatam Sofer took issue,[16] arguing that R. Landau himself had only intended this ruling as a particular exception for those who had to meet important dignitaries on these days, and did not wish his lenient ruling to be promulgated further. Then, the Chatam Sofer writes as follows:

> An individual [halakhic authority], even if he is very great ... should not permit even the smallest [prohibitive] custom of the customs of Israel. For one day he will say such and such and they will publish and publicise it and tomorrow they will say something else with exceedingly weak logical arguments – until they permit a prohibition of the Torah. As indeed has occurred, as a result of our many sins, in our times, that the sinners of the generation are many, and they have argued, 'Look – shaving on *Chol Hamoed* was treated as forbidden for many years by our ancestors ... and now the rabbis have permitted it! Let us also permit public desecration of the Sabbath...' And the responsibility for this will be with those who caused [it]. Thus, the Nodah Bi'Yehudah did not permit it in public, and nevertheless they stumbled [because of his words].[17]

It is clear that the Chatam Sofer was deeply cognizant here of the effect that a lenient ruling in this area could have, certainly an extra-halakhic consideration and one that fits very well with the examples cited above of earlier rulings based upon '*le-migdar miltha*' considerations.[18] Indeed, it was primarily for this reason that he ruled stringently in this area in all circumstances.

Yet, on the same issue, R. Feinstein took a decidedly more lenient approach. After setting out the Talmudic literature on the subject and the opinions of the early commentators, and in particular that of Rabbeinu Tam, R. Feinstein ruled that in his opinion, one who regularly shaves every day (or every few days) would be permitted to do so on

Chol Hamoed as well, as long as he had also shaved on the eve of the festival. His reasoning, in contrast to the Chatam Sofer, was strictly halakhic. The only reason, he argued, that other earlier authorities had disagreed with Rabbeinu Tam on this point was due to the importance of making no distinction in the law in order to avoid confusion (a factor explicitly noted in the Talmud in the context of this issue[19]). Nowadays, however, when the general practice is to shave every weekday, it is perfectly obvious that one who shaves on the intermediate days of the festival does not thereby indicate a neglect to do so on the eve of the festival.

Clearly, the extra-halakhic considerations of the Chatam Sofer, expressed in terms of the impact a leniency in this area could have, should ostensibly play a major part in R. Feinstein's reasoning as well, regardless of the possible grounds for halakhic leniency. Yet, in sharp contrast to the Chatam Sofer, aside for a short note at the very end of the responsum, in which he states that he is only 'accustomed to permit this' to one who has a 'particular need' to do so (thereafter reiterating once again that one should not object to those who wish to be lenient since halakhically it is permitted), he appears not to be troubled by the '*le-migdar miltha*' concerns of the Chatam Sofer at all.

Hence, we are drawn once again to the conclusion that extra-halakhic considerations in terms of the consequences that a ruling may have are very specific to the circumstances within which the ruling is issued. What may have deeply troubled the Chatam Sofer in nineteenth-century Hungary may very well not concern R. Feinstein in twentieth-century America. In their responsa, both seek to rule on a particular issue, taking into account not only the application of earlier sources as well as halakhic precedent, but also the current social circumstances as well as any future implications that a ruling may have. Seen in this light, such differences in outcome are eminently understandable and demonstrate the nuanced and all-rounded approach that a halakhic authority must always take towards his subject matter.

Another significant example of the Chatam Sofer's use of extra-halakhic considerations, and in particular his regard for the consequences of a particular ruling, however justified a practice may be according to the strict letter of the law, is found elsewhere in his responsa. In this piece, he addresses the underlying reasons behind the long-established practice in his day to prohibit, by means of rabbinical decree (known as *cherem*), the re-publication of books by an alternative publishing house for a certain length of time following their initial publication.[20]

As background, R. Moshe Isserlis had argued in an earlier responsum[21] that the basis for issuing such a ban on re-publication was based on the verse, 'Cursed is the one who encroaches [upon] the boundary of his fellow in secret' (Deut. 27:17), from which legislation protecting commercial business rights is generally derived. In dissension from this ruling, the Chatam Sofer argued that the basis for these bans was not this set of laws at all and that according to the strict letter of the law it would in fact not be forbidden for competitive re-publication to take place. Instead, he argued that the source of the practice was extra-halakhic in nature:

> If we would not close the door by preventing such re-publication (i.e. prevent competition), then which fool would enter himself into [a situation in which] he would risk losing several thousands (sic)? The result would be that the whole printing industry [of Jewish works] would stop, Heaven forbid, and the Torah would be lost. Thus, for the benefit of the Jewish people and to exalt the horn of the Torah, our predecessors [instituted] this practice of imposing a fine upon one who encroaches the boundary [of his fellow].[22]

In this instance as well, the Chatam Sofer's treatment of the issue demonstrates his willingness to account for the broader ('extra-halakhic') implications of a particular ruling. Here, this finds application in the justification he gives for a historical practice, even granting it precedence to a potential halakhic source offered by R. Isserlis, due to the fact that he considers the latter to be insufficient in this instance.

In yet another example of this approach, the Chatam Sofer concurs with the ruling of R. Isserlis (cited above)[23] concerning the appointment of a *mamzer* to a position of authority. He concedes that it is true that the Mishnah states that showing respect to a *mamzer* who is a Torah scholar takes precedence over a High Priest who is an ignoramus.[24] Nevertheless, the essentially extra-halakhic consideration that people will refuse to respect his authority as a rabbi due to his situation, means that he should not in practice fill this role. Indeed, writes Chatam Sofer:

> ... how much more so in our generation, where through our many sins the honour of the Torah has been removed and even to those of the most noble pedigree they say, 'remove the beam from between your eyes' (i.e. correct your own faults first). How much so [they will refuse to listen] to the most lowly of families [i.e. the *mamzer*].[25]

R. Feinstein's application of another form of what can be termed an 'extra-halakhic consideration' is also discernible in his responsa. Thus, for instance, in a responsum dated 10 June 1981, he considers the question of whether smoking cigarettes is prohibited according to the halakhah.[26] His conclusion is that since it cannot be proven with certainty that it poses a serious health risk to the majority of people who smoke,[27] it is not subject to the explicit prohibition against injuring oneself. Hence, although strongly advising against it due to the health risks involved, he concludes that in respect of those who do smoke, the verse 'God guards the foolish' (Psalms 116:6) can be invoked.

It is possible that a primary motivation of R. Feinstein in issuing this lenient ruling,[28] despite extensive medical evidence highlighting the danger to health posed by smoking, was motivated by a concern not to issue a ruling that would be near impossible to abide by for those already addicted to smoking. This approach too, has clear precedent in Talmudic law, known as the principle of, 'not decreeing something upon the community unless they are able to withstand it'. Thus, he reserves his strongest language for those who are contemplating starting to smoke, rather than for those who already do so. Having established the fact that halakhic precedent for leniency does in fact exist in this case, based upon the above reasoning, he rules leniently, following this essentially extra-halakhic principle.

There are two further responsa of the Chatam Sofer and R. Feinstein respectively in connection with a different aspect of the synagogue that are particularly important in the context of this discussion. They concern the building of a *mechitzah*, or partition, in order to separate men from women during prayers. In their responsa, both cite the following passage from the Talmud as the source for the requirement to build a *mechitzah*; however, the inferences they extract from it are different.

The relevant passage reads as follows:

> Originally [the walls of the Court of the Women in the Temple] were smooth, but [later the Court] was surrounded with a gallery, and it was enacted that the women should sit above and the men below.
>
> But how could they do so? Is it not written (I Chron. 28:19) 'All this [do I give you] in writing as the Lord has made me wise by His hand upon me' (indicating that prophetic instruction is required in every detail of the Temple's construction)?[29] Rav answered, they found a Scriptural verse and expounded it (Zekh.

> 12:12): 'And the land shall mourn, every family apart'; the family of the house of David apart, and their wives apart. Is it not, they said, an *a fortiori* argument? If in the future when they will be engaged in mourning and the Evil Inclination will have no power over them, the Torah nevertheless says, men separately and women separately, how much more so now when they are engaged in rejoicing and the Evil Inclination has sway over them.[30]

Several points are particularly noteworthy here. In the first instance, although this passage may not be of a strictly aggadic, rather than halakhic, nature, it is apparently describing a historical event that took place in the Temple in Jerusalem, as opposed to providing a formal halakhic ruling regarding the necessity of separating men and women during prayer in the synagogue. Thus, in the context of determining the rules governing a synagogue it certainly would appear to be an unlikely source. Support for this is further borne out by the fact that Maimonides in his halakhic work, Mishnah Torah, does not codify this passage in the section detailing the rules of the synagogue building (Laws of Prayer, chapter 11). The law is instead recorded in two other places, both specifically describing the procedure in the Temple itself. For example, in the Laws of Shofar, Sukkah and Lulav, Maimonides writes as follows:

> What was done? On the eve of the first day of the festival, they would set up a place in the Temple where women [could watch] from above, and men from below, so [that] they would not intermingle with each other.[31]

Nevertheless, both the Chatam Sofer[32] and R. Feinstein[33] cite this passage as the source for the law requiring a *mechitzah* in a synagogue, despite the apparent lack of explicit reference to this in both Maimonides and the other earlier Codes. Furthermore, R. Feinstein asserts that from the details of this passage it is evident that the requirement to install a physical divide in a synagogue between the sexes is Biblical in origin.[34] If this were not so, he argues, the Talmud's query regarding how it could be permissible to alter the design of the Temple (based on the verse in Chronicles) would remain unanswered. The only way to comprehend the manner in which the Talmud resolves this question, according to R. Feinstein, is by understanding the verse in Zekhariah as indicating the existence of a *Biblical* requirement to separate men and women, hence it was as if this too had been prophetically revealed.

For the Chatam Sofer, whose responsum principally discusses the issue of '*kalut rosh*', frivolity that can result from a mixed gathering, leading to the halakhic requirement for separation,[35] this passage provides a source for the qualitative distinction between a place of prayer and that of non-prayer. The proof-text cited by the Talmud from Zekhariah is taken as referring to a family situation: 'And the land shall mourn, every family apart', yet even so the Talmud understands it to mean that 'the family of the house of David [shall mourn] apart, and their wives apart'. Thus, writes the Chatam Sofer:

> Even in a situation in which there would be no problem of an *ervah* (lit. nakedness, a reference to sexual impropriety) prohibition, for instance in the case of one's own wife, nevertheless, in a situation of prayer, thanksgiving or eulogy – whenever one's heart should be turned to God – no improper thoughts should [be allowed] to arise. [Thus] even with one's wife this was said.[36]

Due to the risk of distraction during prayer, separation is deemed necessary according to the Chatam Sofer, even between those whose relationship would not normally have necessitated this.

Thus, we have a fascinating example of a Talmudic passage describing a particular element in the design of the Temple introduced in order to separate the sexes, which is understood by these two later authorities as implying a Biblical requirement to implement this in the synagogue, in all circumstances and even between family members. Once again it is evident from this that the use and application of Talmudic sources in the halakhic process is far from monolithic, and often includes utilizing passages as source-material that would not naturally be viewed as appropriate for such purposes. Crucial to an understanding, therefore, of the path followed by the Chatam Sofer and R. Feinstein in deriving an absolute requirement for a *mechitzah* in a synagogue, is the fact that their application of the sources in question follows a distinct historical tradition also utilized by numerous earlier rabbinic personalities, as demonstrated above.

Especially noteworthy, threfore, are the Chatam Sofer's own words of caution, in another responsum, against the use of certain types of extra-halakhic material in providing a halakhic ruling:

> I am accustomed to say that whoever mixes Kabbalistic topics with established *halakhot* violates the law against sowing mixed seeds: 'lest the ... fruit of the vineyard become sanctified' (Deut. 22:9).

> On the other hand, whoever mixes books of logic (*higgayon*, a reference to rationalistic philosophy) with words of Torah transgresses the law of: 'You shall not plough with an ox and an ass together' (Deut. 22:10). And if he is a leader of the Jewish people, he leads with [forbidden] mixtures.'[37]

Whilst the reference here is specifically to Kabbalistic sources and philosophical concepts, as opposed to aggadic ones, it is nonetheless clear from this brief passage that the Chatam Sofer was of the opinion that great care was to be exercised when issuing, and by extension when verifying the source for, a halakhic ruling.

Further evidence of the importance placed by the Chatam Sofer on ascertaining a verifiable *halakhic* tradition for certain practices, however widespread they may be, is found in another responsum concerning the by then widespread practice of pilgrimage to the grave of the first-century Tannaitic sage R. Shimon bar Yochai on the traditional date of his passing (known as *Lag B'Omer*, after the 33rd day of the *omer* count on which it falls). In questioning the source for this practice, the Chatam Sofer writes as follows:

> Even though all their intentions are for the sake of Heaven, their reward [being] great without doubt ... but to institute a festival on a day up on which no miracle was performed *and is not mentioned in the Talmud and halakhic authorities in any place*, or any hint to it at all, merely a custom to refrain from eulogising and fasting on it, and the reason for this [custom] itself we do not know ... to make it a day of rejoicing and lighting bonfires and in a specific place that will thereby become a pinnacle to which all are drawn – I do not know if it is permissible to do this.[38] (Italics mine)

Here, the Chatam Sofer goes further, making explicit reference to the fact that, in his opinion, in order to be valid, a practice or custom must have a source in the Talmud and halakhic authorities, or at least a hint to one. The more recent *Lag B'Omer* practices he refers to are therefore by definition suspect in his opinion.

Indeed, it is interesting to note that this particular stance regarding not intermingling Kabbalistic tradition with the halakhah was considered by certain other contemporaneous, particularly *chassidic*, rabbinical authorities as *too* conservative in its limitation of potentially valid source material. Thus, for instance, R. Chayyim Elazar Shapira of Munkacs (d.1937), in his responsa *Minchat Elazar*,[39] argues that the Chatam Sofer could not 'God forbid' have 'intended [this] to be taken literally', due to the fact that other important works such as those of R. Abraham Gombiner[40] 'are replete with references' to the Kabbalistic writings.

In a similar vein, R. Feinstein in his introduction to *Iggrot Moshe* emphasizes that the methodology he utilizes in his responsa is reliant upon a very close examination of the source material. The fact that this is so means that:

> ...since I have provided the reasons and all the explanations involved, thus, I am merely as one who teaches the halakhah [in such a way] that the questioner can investigate [the matter] himself, examine it, and make a decision.[41]

Clearly, therefore, the careful use of appropriate source material in determination of the halakhah was of critical importance to both the Chatam Sofer and R. Feinstein, and it is in this light that the above evaluation of their usage of extra-halakhic sources and considerations must be reflected upon.

Conclusion

The process of halakhic decision making, as viewed in the context of the responsa literature in particular, is much wider in scope than may initially appear. Far from being a monolithic process, consisting of a direct application of principles set out in the legalistic sections of the Talmud and the later Codes of Jewish law, in reality it involves a deeply insightful understanding of both the historical and traditional application of the halakha, as well as the ramifications that a particular ruling may have. As Elon observes:

> One of the sources that create Jewish law is legal reasoning, i.e. the reasoning process employed by the halakhic authorities by whom the halakhah is carried forward. This reasoning process is nourished by penetrating insight into the essence of halakhic and legal principles, by an appreciation of human characteristics in social relationships and by a careful study of the real world and its manifestations.
>
> All of these are as appropriate for aggadah as for halakhah, both of which formed the basis upon which the halakhic authorities' thought processes and methods of reasoning were shaped.[42]

In contrast to the argument that, 'their tactic (the ultra-Orthodox) was to expand the reservoir of normative traditions which nourished the halakhic process',[43] the methodology of both the Chatam Sofer and R. Feinstein, seen in the above context, exemplify Elon's depiction of the role that 'legal reasoning' has historically played in the formation of Jewish law. Moreover, their utilization of aggadic passages in a halakhic context where relevant, as well as their careful consideration of the consequences of their decisions, far from being recent innovations, can be demonstrated as having had clear historical precedents from within the corpus of the earlier responsa literature itself.

Both the Chatam Sofer and Rabbi Feinstein were rabbinic leaders *par excellence* who exemplified the ability to ensure the continuity of Jewish tradition in the face of the many and varied challenges to it presented by modernity. This analysis has attempted to demonstrate that it is only through a deeper understanding of the wider processes involved in halakhic decision-making generally that the methodology of these central rabbinical figures in their response to modernity can properly be appreciated.

NOTES

1. R. Moses Sofer, *Sheilot U'Teshuvot Chatam Sofer* (Jerusalem: Machon L'Hotza'at Sefarim V'Cheker Kitvei Yad Al Shem HaChatam Sofer, 2008 [First published Pressburg, Bratislava: Anton Schmidt Printing Press, 1859]), Vol.1, no.28.
2. *bSukkah* 51b, trans. Isidore Epstein (ed.), *The Soncino Talmud* (London: Soncino Press, 1935–1952).
3. As similarly observed by Michael Silber, 'The Emergence of Ultra-Orthodoxy – The Invention of a Tradition', in Jack Wertheimer (ed.), *The Uses of Tradition* (New York: Jewish Theological Seminary of America, 1992), p.53 (n.59).
4. R. Karo evidently understands that this is the reason for the requirement.
5. R. Joseph Karo, *Kesseph Mishneh* (Commentary to Maimonides, Mishnah Torah) (Warsaw: 1880), Laws of Prayer 11:3. His comment is on the seemingly incidental reference made by Maimonides (loc. cit.) to the effect that 'the *bimah* is in the middle'.
6. *Orlah* 3:9, trans. Epstein (ed.), *The Soncino Talmud.*
7. For further discussion and a survey of the instances that this phrase is employed by the Chatam Sofer in his responsa, see Moshe Samet, 'The Beginnings of Orthodoxy', *Modern Judaism* 8, no.3 (1988), pp.249–69 (particularly n.21).
8. *Sheilot U'Teshuvot Chatam Sofer*, Vol.1, no.28.
9. On the effect and ramifications of the *Pesak Din*, see further Jacob Katz, *A House Divided* (Hanover, NH: Brandeis University Press, 1998), pp.56–85, and Silber, 'The Emergence of Ultra-Orthodoxy', pp.50–9.
10. Menachem Elon, *Ha-Mishpat Ha-Ivri: Jewish Law: History Sources and Principles*, trans. by Bernard Auerbach and Melvin Sykes (Philadelphia, PA: Jewish Publication Society, 1994), Vol.1, p.102. See above for further elaboration of Elon's thesis in this area.
11. R. Moshe Feinstein, *Iggrot Moshe* (New York: privately published, 1959–2011), *Orach Chayyim*. Vol.2, no.42.

12. As support for this, R. Feinstein cites the very ruling of R. Joseph Karo mentioned above, who permits it in a case where the synagogue is small and hence the need to place the *bimah* in the middle in order that all can hear clearly is effectively obsolete. This implies that it is not an obligation at all unless the size of the synagogue mandates it (*Iggrot Moshe*, no.41).
13. Lit. to safeguard the matter, see end of Chapter 1.
14. *bMoed Kattan* 17b.
15. R. Judah Landau, *Responsa Nodah Bi'Yehuda, Mahadura Kamma* (Warsaw: 1880, First Edition), *Orach Chayyim*, no.13.
16. *Sheilot U'Teshuvot Chatam Sofer, Orach Chayyim*, no.153.
17. Ibid.
18. See Elon, *Ha-Mishpat Ha-Ivri*, Vol.1, pp.533–6.
19. *bMoed Kattan* 14b.
20. In another responsum (Choshen Mishpat, no.41), the Chatam Sofer traces the origins of this practice to an incident in 1550, in which an edition of Maimonides' *Mishnah Torah* was published by one house, only to be re-published a year later by a rival and sold for a cheaper price. (See further Israel Schneider, 'Jewish Law and Copyright', *Journal of Halacha and Contemporary Society*, 21 (1991), pp.84–96.)
21. R. Moses Isserlis, *Teshuvot Remah* (Jerusalem: Siev, 1971), no.10.
22. *Sheilot U'Teshuvot Chatam Sofer*, Vol.6, no.57.
23. Chapter 2.
24. *mHorayot* 3:8.
25. *Sheilot U'Teshuvot Chatam Sofer*, Even Ha'ezer, Vol.2, no.94.
26. *Iggrot Moshe*, Choshen Mishpat, Vol.2, no.76.
27. Obviously this may well have changed today, due to further advances in medical research in this field.
28. Indeed, several contemporaneous *poskim* to R. Feinstein did in fact consider smoking to be an outright prohibition. See, for instance, R. Eliezer Walldenberg, *Teshuvot Tzitz Eliezer* (Jerusalem: Bloom, 1996), Vol.15, no.39.
29. Cf. *bBaba Bathra* 60b where this principle is applied in order to justify the reason that a permanent ban on eating meat and drinking wine was not instituted following the Temple's destruction, despite the original intention of the Sages to do so.
30. *bSukkah* 51. Trans. Epstein (ed.), *The Soncino Talmud.*
31. *Mishneh Torah*, trans. Eliyahu Touger (New York: Moznaim Publishers, 1997), Laws of Shofar, Sukkah and Lulav, 8:12. This law is also recorded by Maimonides in the Laws of the Chosen House 5:9, concerning the particulars of the Temple design.
32. *Sheilot U'Teshuvot Chatam Sofer*, Choshen Mishpat, Vol.5, no.190.
33. *Iggrot Moshe, Orach Chayyim*, Vol.1, no.39.
34. Ibid.
35. The specific question he was posed concerned whether it would be in order to permit men and women to sing in harmony from opposite sides of the *mechitzah.*
36. *Sheilot U'Teshuvot Chatam Sofer, Choshen Mishpat,* Vol.5, no.190.
37. *Sheilot U'Teshuvot Chatam Sofer, Orach Chayyim*, no.51.
38. Ibid., Yoreh Deah, no.233.
39. R. Chayyim Elazar Shapira, *Responsa Minchat Elazar* (Jerusalem: Ohr Torah Munkatzch, 1996), Vol.2, no.78.
40. Primary commentator on the Shulchan Arukh, known as the Maggen Avraham (d.1682).
41. *Iggrot Moshe, Orach Chayyim*, Vol.1, p.2.
42. Elon, *Ha-Mishpat Ha-Ivri*, Vol.1, p.104.
43. Silber, 'The Emergence of Ultra-Orthodoxy', p.60.

PART II

Response to Science

5

An Overview of Rabbinic Perspectives

The question of the degree of interaction with, and recognition or accommodation of, scientific advancement by proponents of traditional Judaism has a long and fascinating history. Thus, the Jewish response to important scientific advances made during the early modern period has already been the subject of detailed study, as will be outlined below. However, it is the explosion of scientific knowledge within the last hundred years that has arguably caused the greatest challenges yet, in this context, to traditional Judaism. Of particular interest, therefore, is the variety of responses that have arisen to these challenges in recent years. Without seeking to mediate between the various approaches, this section attempts to highlight and contrast several of these responses, as well as examine the degree to which they may possibly reflect that of earlier rabbinic authorities in the early-modern era.

In order to provide an effective framework for an analysis of twentieth-century responses to the challenges of science, it is worthwhile beginning by outlining rabbinic perspectives on science during the early modern period. David Ruderman argues that the interest in medicine and science evident in the works of the great rabbinic personalities of the medieval period, such as Maimonidies, Gersonides and Ibn Ezra, was augmented during the early modern period. In his view, 'the interaction of medicine and science ... was more substantial and repercussive than before'.[1] As an example of this, he cites, amongst others, R. Judah Lowe, the 'Maharal of Prague' (d. 1609), who, according to Ruderman, 'openly encouraged the acquisition of scientific knowledge' and was prepared to engage with science in the context of his works of Torah.[2]

Thus, for example, he discusses Maharal's exposition on the seeming implausibility, from a scientific perspective, of the ability of the sun to stand still for Joshua (see Joshua 10:12–13).[3] According to Maharal, 'it is possible for one subject to possess two opposite conditions because of two perspectives, the course of nature being one unique subject, and the unnatural the other'. What one sees will depend upon which 'realm' a person operates within, the natural (as the rest of the world did) or the miraculous (as did Joshua and his people).[4] For Ruderman, the important point here is that Maharal clearly recognizes the *significance* of science in the context of his explanation of the Torah and the problem that it raises in terms of understanding the miracle of Joshua. His method of dealing with it is to delineate the intrinsic differences between the different 'worlds' that science and Torah operate within. Whether, and to what extent, certain modern rabbinic responses to the challenges of science can be traced to this approach of Maharal is a question that will be considered further below.

An alternative perspective in the early modern period to that of Maharal was suggested by R. Azariah de'Rossi (Mantua, Italy, d.1578), author of the work *Me'or Einayim*.[5] De'Rossi's central argument was that certain aggadic passages in the Talmud must be viewed in the context of later scientific development. In this sense, he attempted to base himself, at least in part, on a viewpoint originally expressed during medieval times. For instance, in *Moreh Nevukhim* (Guide for the Perplexed) 3:14, Maimonidies states:

> You must, however, not expect that everything our Sages say respecting astronomical matters should agree with observation, for mathematics were not fully developed in those days, and their statements were not based on the authority of the Prophets, but on the knowledge which they either themselves possessed or derived from contemporary men of science.[6]

One of de'Rossi's most vociferous opponents, however, was in fact Maharal himself. In his work *Baer HaGolah*[7] he authored a scathing critique of de'Rossi, describing him as someone who:

> ...is unable to understand the words of the Sages ... how can he be unafraid to speak against the Sages ... as if they were people of his generation and friends?[8]

As evident from the example cited above, in outlining Maharal's own approach towards the apparent contradictions presented by science, Maharal's key criticism of de'Rossi is the fact that he *rejects* certain statements of the Sages on account of the science. As an example of this, Maharal cites a passage in the Talmud[9] rejected by de'Rossi due to the fact that it appears consistent with a (scientifically) erroneous view of the earth as being flat rather than spherical.[10] For Maharal, however, the words of the Sages are entirely 'correct', because they were not referring to a physical manifestation at all. They instead referred to the 'essence' of the matter,[11] 'the cause that leads to the natural manifestation',[12] which is by definition a completely different perspective from the scientific one.

Having outlined two significant opposing viewpoints in the early-modern period, it is now possible to consider key twentieth-century rabbinic perspectives on this issue.

It is helpful to preface this section by outlining the three broad categories that these responses can be grouped into. In the first instance, there are those who argue that both the Talmudic and scientific viewpoints can be shown to be entirely accurate, however contradictory they may seem at first. This perspective has clear continuity with that of Maharal outlined above. The second category, broadly entitled '*Torah U'Madda*' (lit. 'Torah and Science'), essentially follows the rationalist school of de'Rossi, arguing that scientifically proven facts must be accepted as such, despite the apparent consequences for the relevant Talmudic passages, for example, in question. The final category of responses questions the grounds for accepting scientific arguments as 'facts' in the first place, arguing instead that they must always be treated as mere hypotheses, as contrasted with the eternal truth of the words of the Sages.

For those rabbinic figures who respond to the issue in the style of the first category, there are three distinct approaches that can be identified, each of which can be traced, in some form, to the argument originally presented by Maharal. The first of these approaches advocates that modern science may necessitate a re-assessment of the *perspective* from which the Talmud analyses or discusses a particular issue. Thus, for example, Rabbi Chaim Friedlander (d.1986) argued that when the Talmud appears to completely contradict modern science, the reason is that the Talmud does not seek to discuss science at all in the first place.[13] Instead, it refers to 'spiritual concepts' which, although couched in physical terms, have no bearing on the physical reality whatsoever. As an example, he cites the essay of Maharal, detailed above, concerning the Sages' descriptions of various astronomical phenomena that appears to be at variance with what is considered elementary science today. In R. Friedlander's view, 'the Sages do not deal with or discuss the external natural sciences, rather [they are discussing] the spiritual sources of nature.'[14]

It is of interest in this context to note that this particular response, namely that science and Torah by definition cannot conflict due to the inherent differences between them, has also been articulated in somewhat different language by some Orthodox Jewish scientists. Thus, for example, Steven Feldstein, a senior research associate at the Earth and Environmental Systems Institute, Pennsylvania State University (writing in *Intercom*, a journal of the Association of Orthodox Jewish Scientists) argues that:

> An awareness of the basics of science – including its methodology and limitations – would show that there doesn't need to be a conflict between the two ... scientific methods, which involve the five senses, cannot be used to investigate these questions. As a result, scientists tend to regard such questions as being beyond the bounds of science. At a very basic level, scientists can only ask 'how' not 'why' about nature's behaviour.[15]

Hence, for Feldstein, the entire *premise* of scientific investigation is intrinsically different to that of the Torah, essentially, the former deals with the 'how' and the latter with the 'why'. The result is that scientific theory cannot, by definition, be used to challenge any aspect of the Torah.

The second of these approaches also argues that science and the Talmud are both correct, but for a different reason. In this view, it is the physical reality of the natural world that has changed, an approach referred to in Hebrew as '*nishtanu ha'tevaiim*', or 'nature has changed'. One of the most well-known proponents of this view was R. Avraham Yeshaya Karelitz (d.1953), popularly known as the Chazon Ish after the title of his most famous work. As a striking example of this approach, he discusses the implication of the Talmud[16] that there are two different 'tubes' present in the male member, one for semen and one for urine.[17] Modern anatomy shows, however, the presence of a single tube, the urethra, that fulfils both functions. This case creates an obvious problem for the initial approach discussed above. The Talmud is referring to a physical anatomical detail, and indeed one that has practical halakhic ramifications.[18] Explaining the Talmud in this context as referring to a 'spiritual concept' is obviously difficult. Instead, the Chazon Ish argues that we are forced to conclude that the physical reality as we see it today is different from that of the time of the Talmud.[19] Our anatomy shows one tube, their anatomy, however was different, consisting of two tubes.[20] This approach is evidently problematic, however, from a scientific perspective. An argument that such major changes in human anatomy have taken place within the last 1,500 years, or thereabouts, appears extremely difficult to comprehend. Indeed, it is for this very reason that other leading rabbinic figures have presented alternative resolutions to this particular problem.[21]

The third approach, within the category of those who seek to potentially allow for the authenticity of both science and the traditionally accepted perspective, has focused its attention on recent cosmological and geological discoveries that appear to contradict the traditional Jewish view. For example, according to the traditional Jewish approach, the universe is less than 6,000 years old, whereas according to science it is some 13 billion years old. In order to resolve this problem, several Jewish theoretical physicists have argued in a similar vein, once again, to that of Maharal, that both are in fact correct, since each are working within different conceptual frameworks. Thus, for instance, Dr Gerald Schroeder, in his book *Genesis and the Big Bang*,[22] argues that Einstein's theory of relativity allows for shifts in the manner in which time itself is measured. Hence, what appears to be millions of years from our perspective, is only days from the perspective of the Torah, 'looking forward', as such, from very different space-time coordinates.[23] It is important to note, however, that Schroeder's ideas have been met with criticism from within the Jewish community itself.[24]

Turning to consider the second category of approaches, other Orthodox scholars, broadly characterized as those subscribing to the '*Torah U'Madda*' (literally, 'Torah and Science') perspective, have responded to the challenge of science differently. In their view, it is incumbent upon believing Jews to seek to deepen their understanding of the Torah within the context that they live, based upon the scientific knowledge currently at their disposal, as indeed the Talmudic Sages themselves did in their day. This approach can be seen as a continuation of that of earlier scholars such as R. Azariah de'Rossi.[25] Rabbi Norman Lamm, former Chancellor of Yeshiva University in New York, is often seen as the 'father' of the *Torah U'Madda* approach.

In a 1971 essay,[26] R. Lamm set out his position vis-à-vis Torah and science in the following way:

> No religious position is loyally served by refusing to consider annoying theories which may well turn out to be facts. Torah is 'a Torah of truth', and to hide from the facts is to distort that truth into a myth. Of course, it must be repeated that the theories here under discussion have not (yet) been established as true. But they may be – and Judaism will then have to confront them as it has confronted what men have considered the truth throughout the generations.
>
> It is this kind of position which honest men, particularly honest believers in God and Torah, must adopt… if they are found to be substantially correct, we may not overlook them. We must then use newly discovered truths the better to understand our Torah – the 'Torah of truth'.[27]

R. Lamm himself stresses here the importance of ascertaining whether or not the science as stated can be confirmed as 'fact'. But in the event that it is proven correct, then, in his view, it must be accepted as such.

On the opposite end of the spectrum from the *Torah U'Madda* approach, is the final category of the three listed above. Those subscribing to this view question the entire basis for what is commonly regarded as 'scientific fact'. Foremost amongst this school of thought is the late Lubavitcher Rebbe, R. Menachem Mendel Schneersohn. In a letter entitled 'Science and Judaism',[28] R. Schneersohn set out his position as follows:

> Science has to do only with theories but not with certainties. All scientific conclusions ... can only be probable in a greater or lesser degree according to the precautions taken in the use of the available evidence, and the degree of probability necessarily decreases with the distance from the empirical facts.[29]

It is important to emphasise that R. Schneersohn himself asserts that his approach is not based upon casting 'aspersions on the scientific method' itself.[30] Instead he argues that there is a 'misconception' about the scientific method.[31] Since scientific theory relies upon either interpolation or extrapolation, neither of which can be stated with absolute certainty, certain assumptions and calculations must always be made. Hence, in his view, 'there *can* be no real conflict between any scientific theory and the Torah'.[32] Torah represents truth whereas science deals with theory.

By way of conclusion, without seeking to mediate between the different views, this section has sought to provide an overview of the variety of rabbinic responses to challenges posed by science in the twentieth century. It has also explored the possible links between these responses and certain historical approaches taken towards these issues in the early-modern period. Whilst the modern responses vary considerably in both content and style, all demonstrate a desire to respond to these challenges in a clear and coherent manner, yet remain true to traditional Jewish teachings. It is this, above all, that has a clear historical precedent – from the Talmud itself, through the medieval and early modern periods until today.

NOTES

1. David B. Ruderman, *Jewish Thought and Scientific Discovery in Early Modern Europe* (New Haven, CT: Yale University Press, 1995), p.10.
2. Ibid. As evidence of the former, Ruderman (p.78) cites R. Judah Lowe, *Netivot Olam, Netiv Hatorah* (Bnei Brak: Yahadut Publications, 1980), p.60: 'study of the sciences that focus on reality and the order of the world is certainly permitted ... They are like a ladder to ascend to the science of Torah.'
3. R. Judah Lowe, *Sefer Gevurot Hashem* (New York: Judaica Press, 1969), pp.15–16, cited in Ruderman, *Jewish Thought and Scientific Discovery*, p.79.
4. Ibid.
5. Translated with introduction and annotations by Joanna Weinberg, *Azariah de' Rossi, The Light of the Eyes* (New Haven, CT: Yale University Press, 2001). First published Mantua 1573–75.
6. *Guide For the Perplexed*, trans. M. Friedlander (London: Routledge & Kegan Paul Ltd, 1904), p.278.
7. R. Judah Lowe (Maharal), *Baer HaGolah* (Israel: Books Export Enterprises Ltd, 1980), pp.126–41.
8. Ibid., p.127.
9. *bTam*. 32a.
10. 'Alexsandrous asked the Elders of the Negev: Which is the greater distance – from the heavens to the earth or from the east to the west.'
11. Maharal, *Baer HaGolah*, p.128.
12. Ibid., p.106.
13. R. Chaim Friedlander, *Siftei Chaim Vol.2* (based on notes taken from a recorded lecture) (Bnei Brak: 1997), pp.143–54.
14. Ibid., p.154.
15. S. Feldstein, 'Science & Torah: Can They Go Hand In Hand?', *Intercom*, XXVI, no.1 (2006), p.1.
16. *bYeb.* 75b.
17. The Talmud discusses the case of a man whose semen tube became 'blocked' and discharged semen through the urine tube.
18. See for instance, *b.Bek* 44b: 'when a person needs [to urinate] if one [of the tubes] ruptures into the other, he becomes sterile'. The Talmud therefore requires a man to exercise caution in not delaying a need to urinate.

19. R. Avraham Yeshaya Karelitz, *Chazon Ish Even HaEzer* (Bnei Brak: 1991), 12:7.
20. Nevertheless, according to Chazon Ish elsewhere (ibid 27:3), it appears that the halakha in such cases would remain as formulated in the Talmud, for reasons he sets out in detail.
21. See for instance Responsa *Cheshev Haephod* 2:8, quoted in *Nishmat Avraham*, Even Ha'ezer 5:3. See also R. Dr Mordechai Halperin, *Erectile Dysfunction and Male Infertility*, Dr. Falk Schlesinger Institute for Medical-Halachic Research, http://98.131.138.124/articles/FIC/20.asp (accessed 13 April 2015).
22. Gerald L. Schroeder, *Genesis and the Big Bang* (New York: Bantam, 1990), pp.49–52.
23. Ibid.
24. See, for instance, Yoram Bogacz, 'Genesis & The Big Bluff', Torah Explorer, 20 March 2012, http://torahexplorer.com/genesis-and-the-big-bluff/, a critique of Schroeder (both on scientific and theological grounds) by an Orthodox rabbi.
25. Cf. Ruderman, *Jewish Thought and Scientific Discovery*, p.80.
26. R. Norman Lamm, 'The Religious Implication of Extra-terrestrial Life', in A. Carmell and C. Domb (eds), *Challenge: Torah Views on Science and Its Problems* (New York: Feldheim Publishers, 1978), pp.354–98.
27. Ibid., pp.369–70.
28. R. Menachem M. Schneersohn, 'A Letter on Science and Judaism', in A. Carmell and C. Domb (eds), *Challenge: Torah Views on Science and Its Problems* (New York: Feldheim Publishers, 1978), pp.142–9.
29. Ibid., p.149.
30. Ibid.
31. Ibid., p.146.
32. Ibid., p.149.

PART III
Response to Tragedy

6

Introduction: Spiritual Resistance - Rabbinic Leadership during the Holocaust

Warsaw, Kovno and Vilna were all major Jewish population centres in pre-war Eastern Europe. Life within the ghettos established by the Nazis in these cities is therefore central to any study of Jewish life in general under the Nazis. Importantly, in this context, is the fact that a significant proportion of the Jewish population in these cities were 'religious', in the sense that the preservation of Jewish law, religious thought, tradition and custom was of central importance to them. This section seeks to analyse the nature of rabbinic leadership in these ghettos and the way in which they provided guidance to their communities under the most unimaginably difficult circumstances. In particular, it will focus on the extent to which the preservation and continuity of religious traditions in the ghettos included in this study, led by their rabbinic personalities, was intended to be, or can possibly be viewed as, a form of resistance to the Nazis. Of necessity, therefore, the first section of this analysis will examine the scholarly debate within Holocaust historiography itself surrounding the definition of 'Jewish resistance' under the Nazis.

'Jewish Resistance' in the context of the Holocaust is a term that has been the subject of considerable controversy during the post-war era. For some, such as Raul Hilberg,[1] 'resistance' can only refer to some form of armed struggle. This, essentially, is the more 'traditional' image of resistance that has its roots in the words and actions of Jewish partisans such as Abba Kovner, during and in the immediate aftermath of the Holocaust. Thus, for example, in Kovner's famous pamphlet calling for resistance, first published in Vilna on 13 December 1941, he implored his fellow Jews not to be led 'like sheep to the slaughter'.

Furthermore, as stressed by Michael Marrus in his 1987 survey of Holocaust historiography, early perspectives on resistance were certainly influenced by a preoccupation with a need to, 'right the historical balance – [by] establishing the importance of Jewish heroism in the face of overwhelming force'.[2] There was an 'unspoken assumption' in the eyes of many, according to Marrus, that 'Jewish resistance somehow validates Jewish self-worth', and in this sense what was implied was clearly armed resistance. Perhaps the greatest proof of this was the official title given to the day designated by the Israeli government in 1951 as Holocaust Remembrance Day (known in Hebrew as *Yom HaShoah*), 'Holocaust and *Heroism* Remembrance Day', and the fact that the date chosen for this event, 27 Nissan according to the Hebrew calendar, was selected due to its proximity to the anniversary of the Warsaw Ghetto Uprising.

A consequence of the adoption of this position however, was to argue, as Hilberg asserts, that the Jews' 'reaction pattern … .[was] characterised by almost complete lack of resistance'.[3] According to Hilberg, the Jews had a tendency to 'automatically comply' with German orders, the greatest representation of this seen in the *Judenrat*, the Jewish councils set up by the Nazis to manage Jewish populations in cities throughout occupied Europe. Hilberg considers their policy as being one of 'institutional compliance', becoming mere 'implements of German will'. Indeed, if Jewish resistance is to be measured in terms of the numbers of Germans killed or wounded by Jews, it is true to say, according to Hilberg, that, 'in the totality of the destruction process it was of no consequence'.[4]

Of particular note, however, when considering Hilberg's position in the context of this discussion, is the qualification he makes in the introduction to his book. Hilberg writes that his depiction of a totally submissive victim and a near total lack of resistance on the part of the Jews:

> …refers only to ghetto Jews. This reaction pattern was born in the ghetto and it will die there. It is part and parcel of ghetto life. It applies to all ghetto Jews – assimilationists and Zionists, the capitalists and the socialists, the unorthodox and the religious.[5]

It is precisely this perception of the 'ghetto Jew' that this section seeks to analyse and present a critique of, based on the evidence relating to religious life and thought in the ghettos.

Hilberg's work and his view of a 'total lack of resistance' on the part of Jews in the ghettos has been subjected to, in Marrus' words, 'a firestorm of criticism',[6] in a large part due to its narrow definition of what constituted 'resistance' in the context of the Holocaust. As a result, many scholars have subsequently argued for a more inclusive approach when considering the definition of 'Jewish resistance'. Perhaps the leading exponent of this school of thought is the Israeli Holocaust scholar Yehuda Bauer. In his definition, 'resistance' is:

> ...any *group* action consciously taken in opposition to known or surmised laws, actions, or intentions directed against the Jews by the Germans and their supporters (emphasis in original).[7]

For Bauer, the key measuring stick by which resistance should be assessed is not so much the effect that it had on the Nazi oppressors, but the perspective taken by the persecuted themselves. This subjective approach to 'resistance' leads to a far greater number of people who can be said to have taken steps towards resisting the Nazis. Indeed, Bauer goes so far as to state that simply keeping 'body and soul' together during the suffering of the Holocaust was a form of resistance.[8] Thus, in a 1998 interview conducted by Amos Goldberg under the auspices of Yad Vashem,[9] Bauer argued that Kovner's words (cited above) had been taken out of context and mistakenly applied as a highly demeaning post-war criticism of the vast majority of Holocaust victims who indeed appeared to go, 'like sheep to the slaughter'. In reality, according to Bauer, Kovner meant it as a rallying cry in the sense of, 'let us not go like sheep to the slaughter!' In using that metaphor, Kovner intended to rebel *against* its very use, not to suggest that he saw himself and others as in fact acting like 'sheep'.

In the same interview, Bauer explained that, in his view, resistance could take many forms and its actual impact on the enemy was in fact irrelevant:

> They did this by fighting physically against the Germans, and by any kind of reaction in-between – from maintaining schools and prayer groups, to organising literary and artistic presentations – because the perception was that the Nazis wanted to destroy the morale of the Jewish population.

> Whether this perception was true or not makes no difference. In opposition to a perceived German threat against the morale of the Jews, the Jewish population reacted by maintaining its cultural, educational and religious dignity.[10]

Importantly, Bauer also stressed the fact that in circumstances where the victim had a certain ideological standpoint, whether religious, Zionist or other, this gave them the strength to, 'not just accept what was being done but to react'.[11]

Clearly, however, Bauer's definition of the term 'resistance' is extremely wide, and it is for this reason that other scholars such as Michael Marrus propose a modification of Bauer's view, yet without limiting the definition of resistance to the armed variety. For Marrus, resistance means:

> ...organized activity consciously intended to damage the persecutors of Jews or *seriously impair their objectives* ... what matters, from this standpoint, is less what was accomplished than the intent of striking a blow against the Nazi machine (emphasis added).[12]

In explaining what particular actions would qualify as 'resistance' under this definition, Marrus cites Emmanuel Ringelblum, leader of the put '*Oyneg Shabes*' underground group in the Warsaw Ghetto as an example. In June 1942, Ringelblum wrote that the achievement of smuggling to London details of the extermination of Polish Jewry had 'struck the enemy a hard blow'.[13] Marrus argues that the fact that the massive Allied retaliatory attacks against the Nazis that Ringelblum expected as a result of his efforts were not in fact forthcoming, and that the persecution continued unabated, was irrelevant. The clear *goal* of Ringelblum and his associates was to resist the Nazis in a way that they felt able to at the time. Thus, concludes Marrus, the 'best yardstick for identifying Jewish resistance is that which the Jews at the time were prepared to accept'.[14]

With this introduction in mind, it is now possible to consider various examples of rabbinic leadership in the ghettos and analyse whether their activities, together with the activities of their communities, can be viewed as a form of 'resistance', under the wider definition of the term proposed by scholars such as Bauer and Marrus. In terms of general background to this topic, the work of Moshe Prager, a follower of the Gerer Rebbe who escaped together with the Rebbe from Poland to Palestine in the early 1940s, is highly insightful. Prager collated anecdotes, stories and ghetto songs, which were often focused on themes of 'spiritual resistance' similar to those discussed in this chapter. Later he published them in a variety of works in both Hebrew and Yiddish, several of which were later translated into English, in books such as *Those Who Never Yielded*.[15] A survey of Prager's works is beyond the scope of this study, but will be helpful for those who wish to investigate the topic further.

NOTES

1. R. Hilberg, *The Destruction of the European Jews* (New York: Holmes & Meier, 1985, rev. edn), III,.
2. M. Marrus, *The Holocaust in History* (New York: Meridian, 1987), p.136.
3. Hilberg, *The Destruction of the European Jews*, pp.1030–1. Cited in Marrus, *The Holocaust in History*, p.136.
4. Ibid.
5. Hilberg, *The Destruction of the European Jews*, p.27.
6. Marrus, *The Holocaust in History*, p.109. In particular, Marrus cites Nathan Eck's 'Historical Research or Slander?', *Yad Vashem Studies* 6 (1967), pp.385–430. In this article, Eck argues that Hilberg's work was 'not a serious study', but a 'slander on the Jews'.
7. Y. Bauer, *They Chose Life: Jewish Resistance in the Holocaust* (New York: Amer Jewish Committee, 1973), p.33. Marrus, *The Holocaust in History*, p.137.
8. Ibid.
9. Amos Goldberg, Interview with Yehuda Bauer, Shoah Resource Centre, Yad Vashem, Jerusalem, 18 January 1998, pp.30, 31.
10. Ibid., p.25.
11. Ibid., p.26.
12. Marrus, *The Holocaust in History*, pp.137–8.
13. Jacob Sloan (ed. and trans.), *Notes From The Warsaw Ghetto: The Journal of Emmanuel Ringelblum* (New York: Schocken, 1986), p.295.
14. Marrus, *The Holocaust in History*, p.138.
15. Moshe Prager, *Those Who Never Yielded* (Wisconsin: Lightbooks, 1980).

7

Warsaw

In the context of the Warsaw Ghetto, the largest of all the ghettos established by the Nazis in occupied Europe, the writings and evidence provided by two key religious personalities of the ghetto will be examined, those of Rabbi Shimon Huberband and Rabbi Kalonymus Kalman Shapiro, the Piaseczner Rebbe.

Shimon Huberband (1909–42) was a member of Emmanuel Ringelblum's *Oyneg Shabes* archive group. This extraordinary group of people living in the Warsaw Ghetto devoted almost all their energies, under the most challenging of circumstances, towards providing an accurate historical record of the destruction of Polish Jewry. Due to Huberband's status as an Orthodox rabbi he was, in the words of Samuel Kassow, in his book on the Archive, 'indispensible to the *Oyneg Shabes* as a conduit to the religious community'.[1] He was also seen by his more secular colleagues as entirely objective in his factually accurate accounts of religious life in the ghetto, something they admired greatly.[2] Indeed, Iwona Irwin-Zarecka and Simcha Fishbane in their review of Huberband's posthumously published book, *Kiddush Hashem: Jewish Religious and Cultural Life in Poland*,[3] bemoan the fact that Huberband did not disclose how he as a rabbi felt during the period he was writing about. Whilst recognising the fact that Huberband is to be admired for his detached, scholarly approach to his subject matter, they felt that it would nonetheless have been invaluable if a detailed account had been left of how a religious Jew 'thought and felt' in the Warsaw Ghetto.[4]

Nevertheless, Huberband's work and its contribution to the historiography of the Holocaust is vital in its portrayal of how the response of significant numbers of religious Jews to Nazi atrocities was often characterized by an even stronger devotion to their faith. In *Kiddush Hashem*, Huberband compiled numerous stories of 'martyrs', those who died 'in sanctification of God's Name'. Huberband's definition of how a *Kiddush Hashem* could be 'performed' provides an important backdrop for the numerous accounts that he and others recorded of such events. In his view it could be performed in one of three ways:

> A. a Jew sacrifices his life when others attempt to make him abandon his Jewish faith. B. a Jew gives his life to save a fellow Jew, and even more so – to save a group of Jews. C. a Jew dies while fighting to defend other Jews. Maimonides rules that if a Jew is killed, even without any overt attempt to make him abandon the Jewish faith, but because he is a Jew, he is considered a martyr.[5]

Thus, for instance, Huberband related the story of a rabbi who refused to tear apart a Torah scroll despite a Nazi order to do so, and as a consequence was burnt alive together with the scroll.[6] Huberband's purpose in compiling these stories was not, as stated previously, to 'defend' religious Jewry from the charges of many, Ringelblum included, who claimed that Orthodox Jews showed much less willingness to die for '*Kiddush Hashem*' than they had in previous eras of persecution. He simply wished to compile, for the historical record, the many instances that he discovered of those that in fact did do so.[7]

The importance of his account in the context of this discussion, as emphasized by Kassow,[8] is the significant number of individual examples it provides of how the faith of numerous Jews within the religious community of the ghetto helped them to, 'face death with dignity and quiet courage'. Thus, for instance, Kassow cites as an example Huberband's account of a certain Yosef Peykus, who, sentenced to death for leaving the ghetto, managed to write a final letter to his wife, containing an ethical will for their son. A deep faith and resultant sense of equanimity amongst the victims involved emerges from reading these stories.

However, it is important to note in assessing the content of Huberband's accounts, that the majority are of individuals, as opposed to entire communities. Individual acts such as these can certainly be considered acts of 'resistance' in the sense that they provided a means to both survive and protest Nazi attempts to crush the spirit of their victims. Nevertheless, returning to Bauer's definition of resistance as outlined above, it is necessary to look at religious communities or religious social groups as a whole in order to assess the extent that, '*group* action [was] consciously taken in opposition to known or surmised laws, actions, or intentions directed against the Jews by the Germans'.[9]

In this context, the influence of Rabbi Kalonymus Kalman Shapiro, the Piaseczner Rebbe (of whom Huberband himself was a close confident) is highly significant. Rabbi Shapiro (1889–1943) was a spiritual leader of a particular sect of Chassidic Jews living in the Warsaw Ghetto. Shortly before he was himself deported to the death camps, he managed to conceal under the floor of his house a collection of his weekly sermons, which were later discovered and published in Israel in 1960 under the title *Eish Kodesh*, meaning 'Holy Fire'.[10] They are one of the most important works to survive the Holocaust, as argued by Henry Abramson in his assessment of the psychological impact of Rabbi Shapiro on his followers,[11] because of the insight they provide 'in real time' of how his community dealt with and reacted to the Nazi oppression on a week-by-week basis. Crucially, they are not a 'memoir', subject to possible distortions of memory, but were disseminated orally to the Rebbe's followers. The numbers who came to hear Rabbi Shapiro's sermons were also clearly not insignificant. Huberband records in his diary, for instance, that a gathering in June 1940 attracted some 150 people.[12]

Of particular significance are the psychological strategies, based on his religious teachings, that Rabbi Shapiro encouraged his followers to adopt in order to deal with the catastrophe they were engulfed in. The Rebbe did not attempt to escape the reality of the situation in his sermons. Indeed, as Abramson points out,[13] the topic of suffering is the primary theme in 43 of the 87 sermons collected in *Eish Kodesh* and a secondary theme in another 18. A key subject of these discussions about suffering often addresses the fact that in the circumstances the community found itself, it was nearly impossible to achieve a degree of *simcha*, joy, something that was particularly important to the Chassidic way of life in general.

Instead, based on Talmudic teachings, the Rebbe sought to help ease the suffering[14] by reference to, firstly, the fact that the suffering of every individual Jew was itself of 'cosmic significance'; secondly, that 'God Himself suffers with every Jew'; and thirdly, that the primary response of the Chassid must be a radical acceptance of the Divine will. Importantly, the Rebbe never refers in his discourses to the Nazis by name. Instead, he sees the suffering of the Jews in the Holocaust as an event of metaphysical proportions. In his view, the hatred of the Jews by the Nazis was not a result of economic or social factors, but a 'supernatural hatred emanating from a diabolical source'.[15]

The effect this viewpoint, consistently reinforced in his sermons, would likely have had on his Chassidic following is seen by Abramson as highly significant:

> By removing the discussion from the mundane political concerns of the day and placing it in a cosmic context, Rabbi Shapiro affirms the intense reality of the suffering while simultaneously elevating its importance. The suffering Chassid is not an insignificant pawn in a large human war, oppressed by the mighty and powerful. He is a holy warrior fighting *with his suffering* for all that is sacred in the universe.[16]

The most important feature of '*Eish Kodesh*' is specifically the fact that it was not intended to serve as a work to be studied by scholars in a library. On the contrary, it was a 'user's document, intended to strengthen the individual Chassid in his weakening personal piety and to reinforce the social dynamic of the embattled Chassidic community'.[17]

What is of particular interest in the context of this discussion is the direct challenge, in a polemical sense, this represented to Nazi attempts to dehumanize the persecuted Jewish people in the ghetto. Much of the oppressive Nazi laws that governed day to day life in the ghetto were intended to psychologically 'break' the spirit of the Jews and to lead them to the self-conclusion that they were in fact sub-human. Thus, it can be argued that Rabbi Shapiro's teachings certainly constituted a form of 'resistance' to the Nazis under Bauer's formulation, in the sense that the Chassidic community that he led, so determined to preserve and elevate its spirits through his theological lessons, clearly constituted a 'group action consciously taken in opposition' to Nazi attempts at dehumanisation.[18] For Rabbi Shapiro, the greatest possible form of resistance to the Nazis was by 'accepting it' as an expression of the Divine will.

Clearly, however, this form of 'resistance' would have remained largely limited to the psychological level. In order to consider other forms of resistance to the Nazis, specific to the religious populations of the ghettos and their rabbinic leadership, we will therefore now turn to life in the Kovno Ghetto.

NOTES

1. S. Kassow, *Who Will Write Our History? Rediscovering A Hidden Archive From The Warsaw Ghetto* (New York: Vintage, 2007), p.167.

2. Ibid.
3. Shimon Huberband, *Kiddush Hashem: Jewish Religious and Cultural Life in Poland*, ed. and trans. by Jeffrey S. Gurock and Robert S. Hirt (New York: Ktav Publishing House Inc., 1987).
4. Iwona Irwin-Zarecka and Simcha Fishbane, Review of Shimon Huberband, *Kiddush Hashem: Jewish Religious and Cultural Life in Poland, Holocaust and Genocide Studies*, 4, no.3 (1989), pp.382–4.
5. Huberband, *Kiddush Hashem*, p.247.
6. Ibid., p.254.
7. Kassow, *Who Will Write Our History?*, p.168.
8. Ibid., p.169.
9. Yehuda Bauer, *They Chose Life: Jewish Resistance in the Holocaust* (New York: Amer Jewish Committee, 1973), p.33.
10. Kalonymus Kalman Shapiro, *Eish Kodesh* (Jerusalem: Feldheim Publishers, 2007, rev. edn). For an account of the life of Rabbi Shapiro, see Nehemia Polen, *The Holy Fire, the Teachings of Rabbi Kalonymus Kalman Shapira, the Rebbe of the Warsaw Ghetto* (Maryland: Jason Aronson, 1994).
11. Henry Abramson, 'The Esh Kodesh of Rabbi Kalonimus Kalmish Shapiro: A Chassidic Treatise on Communal Trauma from the Holocaust', *Journal of Transcultural Psychiatry*, 37 (2000), pp.321–35.
12. Quoted in ibid.
13. Ibid., p.325.
14. Following Abramson's analysis of the sermons, ibid., p.329.
15. Shapiro, *Eish Kodesh*, p.21.
16. Abramson, 'The Esh Kodesh of Rabbi Kalonimus Kalmish Shapiro', p.330.
17. Ibid., p.323.
18. Bauer, *They Chose Life*, p.33.

8

Kovno

Kovno, or Kaunas in Lithuanian, as the capital city of Lithuania, had a Jewish population of about 40,000 during the interwar years. At its peak, the ghetto established by the Nazis to hold the Jews of the city following the invasion of Soviet Russia in June 1941 held a similar number. One of the most important accounts of life in the Kovno Ghetto under the Nazis is that of Rabbi Ephraim Oshry (1914–2003), a well-known rabbi who had studied under the great rabbinic sages of Lithuania. In 1951 he published in Yiddish his account of the period, entitled *Churbin Lita*, later translated into English under the title *The Annihilation of Lithuanian Jewry*.[1] Oshry's other major work, also of significant value to this analysis, was his *Sheilot Uteshuvot Mima'amakim,* or 'Questions and Answers from the Depths'.[2] This was a collection of Oshry's own responses to questions of Jewish law and ethics that had been posed to him during the war in order to provide a ruling. When Oshry went into hiding in 1944, he buried them in milk cans, which he later retrieved after the liberation. The first of these volumes was published in Hebrew in 1959, and it was subsequently followed by four further volumes, with the final one appearing in 1979. In 1983, Oshry published an abridged single volume edition in English, based on the original Hebrew work, under the title *Responsa From The Holocaust*.[3]

Oshry's stated aim in writing his account was to, 'raise a monument to destroyed Lithuanian Jewry, to ... the *gaonim* [great ones] and *tzadikkim* [righteous ones]'.[4] In describing the manner in which many religious Jews in Kovno went to their deaths, Oshry emphasised that:

> These are not mere reports of murder, rather they are holy pages of Jewish martyrology, of *Kiddush Hashem*. Jews did not merely

> die, they sanctified G-d. They fought for Jewish honour and worth.[5]

In this sense, Oshry saw the importance of his work in a similar way to Shimon Huberband in Warsaw. By providing accounts of the many instances of '*Kiddush Hashem*', as he put it, Oshry wished to demonstrate the extreme piety and deep reservoirs of faith that inhabitants of the ghetto possessed.

However, it is Oshry's account of the manner in which these inhabitants of the ghetto sought to preserve their way of life and traditions in the face of such overwhelming oppression that is most instrumental in illustrating how this constituted a form of 'group resistance' to the Nazis. Thus, for instance, Oshry describes in detail how, upon learning of a German plan on 18 February 1942 to destroy the holy books of the Jews, a group of individuals removed all the holy volumes and Torah scrolls from Kovno's synagogues and hid them from the Germans, protecting them with their lives.[6] Similarly, Oshry recounts the superhuman efforts that the community went to in order to obtain the Four Species and *Sukkah* (booth) required for the Festival of Tabernacles[7] and in baking *matzah* (unleavened bread) for Passover.[8]

Elsewhere, Oshry describes the lengths that the religious community in Kovno went to in order to ensure that their educational institutions would continue to function. Thus, for example, the *Tiferes Bachurim* organization, which existed throughout Lithuania in order to provide a meeting place for young religious working men to be able to study Torah together, decided that they would try and obtain facilities within the confines of the Kovno Ghetto.[9] Once they had found the required premises, they worked hard at making the room suitable for study and installed the necessary furniture. Since the entire operation was completely outlawed by the Germans, however, they also constructed a hiding place near the Ark in which they could hide if they were discovered during prayer or study.

Oshry then relates how, upon completion of the study room, they celebrated its dedication, and notes how, 'all the factions in the ghetto recognised and praised this achievement'.[10] According to Oshry, even the Chief of the Second District Jewish Police guarded the area during the celebration in case the Germans interrupted them. This is significant, as it serves to underline the fact that the perseverance of rabbinic leadership in seeking to protect and preserve the religious traditions of their communities would also occasionally receive the admiration of their secular counterparts, and thus become a source of wider inspiration for all. In Oshry's own words, assessing the significance of these actions:

> Repeating this tragic number (six million) does not tell anyone how these Jews died or – what is perhaps more significant – how they lived until they died ... In the purely physical aspects of the confrontation, the Germans did ... succeed ... Physically we were not able to resist. But the Jewish spirit never broke.[11]

It is this strength and resolve, illustrated so vividly by Oshry, of a community determined to maintain its traditions and community infrastructure at all costs, through defying German attempts to prevent all forms of religious observance in the ghetto, which provides a vehicle for translating their actions into a form of 'group resistance'.

In a 1998 review of Oshry's work,[12] Eric Sterling described how in this sense it complimented that of Alex Faitelson's, *Heroism and Bravery in Lithuania 1941–1945*.[13] Faitlelson's account of the same period and locality focuses on the military resistance of the Kovno ghetto and the surrounding partisans, stemming from Faitelson's own membership of the Anti-Fascist Fighting Organisation (AKO) of the Kovno ghetto. As Sterling observes:

> ...the books complement each other, illustrating how Jews suffering the same hardships in the same ghetto employed different approaches – one military and the other spiritual – in the fight for Jewish survival.[14]

For Sterling, the intensity with which that spiritual battle for survival was waged by the Jews of Kovno is well illustrated by Oshry's description of his own encounter with the ghetto liquidator, *SS Scharfuhrer* Bruno Kittel. Oshry was baking *matzah* for Passover when Kittel entered. Realizing that it was too late to hide, Oshry recalled thinking that 'if he was going to die, let it at least be for the *mitzvah* (commandment) of baking *matzah*'.[15] He began to recite the '*Viduy*' confessional prayer recited before death, but was interrupted by Kittel asking him who he was. Before he had a chance to answer, however, Kittel picked up two parcels of *matzah* and walked out. Although this left Oshry with only a small amount of *matzah* for the festival, he set about dividing it into as many required olive-sized pieces as possible, so that more people could fulfil the *mitzvah*.

This 'spiritual' fight against the Nazi killing machine is also profoundly demonstrated in Oshry's other literary product of his years in the Kovno Ghetto, *Sheilot Uteshuvot Mima'amakim*. In his introduction to the abbreviated English version of this work, entitled *Responsa From the Holocaust*, Oshry explained his purpose in publishing what was essentially a book of Jewish law in English. He stated that he desired to:

> ...add to the records of history my own experience of how the victims of Nazi murderers demonstrated their superiority to the 'master race' by clinging to G-d and to His Law ... [these were] questions asked by ordinary Jews who refused to be turned into instinctive animals in search of bare survival.[16]

As detailed above, the Jewish tradition of taking questions to a rabbi for guidance in matters of religious law had a long and glorious history, particularly amongst the Orthodox population of Lithuania with its famous *yeshivot*, or academies of religious learning. The nature of the questions that were brought to Rabbi Oshry during the war, however, demonstrate simultaneously both the tenacity of his community in their adherence to their faith as well as the horrendously tragic situation in which they found themselves.

Thus, for instance, Oshry was asked to rule on the permissibility of performing an abortion in the ghetto, on whether cremation was permissible to avoid burial among gentiles, and on the permissibility of using the garments of martyred Jews. He was asked whether it would be allowed to risk one's life in order to join the partisans, whether items stolen from the Germans could be used in order to fulfil religious requirements and what blessing would be appropriate to recite before martyrdom at the hands of the Nazis. For Oshry, as stated in his introduction, the remarkable inner strength that prompted Jews to ask these questions was their greatest response to the Nazi terror:

> The enemy robs and kills, and Jews, knowing that they are being killed only because they are Jews, sanctify G-d in going to their deaths, wanting to die with the correct words on their lips, because a Jew, who sanctifies every atom of life, sanctifies death as well; and a martyr's death must be accompanied by the correct blessing.[17]

Oshry rails against those who sought after the war to 'salvage' from the ghetto 'sentimental curiosities' such as a burnt page of the Talmud in order to put them in a museum.[18] The greatest way of immortalizing the memory of the victims was, in his view, through demonstrating their strength of spirit. He emphasizes that the people asking these questions were not 'wonderworking rabbis ... who secretly and humbly had mastered the Talmud and Kabbalah, but simple Jews whose faith in the Almighty was the core of their being'.[19] It was, according to Oshry, specifically when they realized that they were the target of the Germans, 'just because they were Jews – that our Jewishness was being attacked – then our Jewish pride came to the fore'.[20]

This was arguably more than what Bauer termed the 'keeping of body and soul together' as a form of resistance.[21] This was a resistance to Nazism through the preservation of the very religion and way of life they attempted to destroy. The deeply held religious beliefs of these communities and their rabbinic leaders gave them the strength, as noted by Bauer,[22] to cope with and resist the Nazi terror.

NOTES

1. Ephraim Oshry, *The Annihilation of Lithuanian Jewry* (New York: The Judaica Press Inc., 1995).
2. Ephraim Oshry, *Sheilot Uteshuvot Mima'amakim* (Heb. 5 vols) (New York: Modern Linotype Co., 1959–79).
3. Ephraim Oshry, *Responsa From The Holocaust* (New York: The Judaica Press Inc., 1983).
4. Oshry, *The Annihilation of Lithuanian Jewry*, Introduction, p.i.
5. Ibid., p.5.
6. Ibid., pp.71–7.
7. Ibid., p.53.
8. Ibid., pp.80–4.
9. Ibid., p.88.
10. Ibid.
11. Ibid., pp.71–2.
12. Eric Sterling, 'Review of *The Annihilation of Lithuanian Jewry*', *Journal of Holocaust and Genocide Studies*, 12 (1998), pp.158–61.
13. Alex Faitelson, *Heroism and Bravery in Lithuania 1941–1945* (Jerusalem: Gefen, 1996).
14. Sterling, 'Review of *The Annihilation of Lithuanian Jewry*', p.158.
15. Oshry, *The Annihilation of Lithuanian Jewry*, p.84.
16. Ibid., Foreword.
17. Ibid., p.xiv.
18. Ibid., p.x.
19. Ibid., pp.xii–xiii.
20. Ibid.
21. Yehuda Bauer, *They Chose Life: Jewish Resistance in the Holocaust* (New York: Amer Jewish Committee, 1973).
22. Yehuda Bauer, 'Interview With Yehuda Bauer – January 18th 1998'. Shoah Resource Centre, Yad Vashem, Jerusalem, http://www1.yadvashem.org/odot, p.26.

9

Vilna

Vilna, or Vilnius in Lithuanian, was home to some 60,000 Jews at the outbreak of the war in 1939. Although this number was far less than, for example, the number of Jews living in Warsaw at the time, the Jewish inhabitants of the city saw themselves, as noted by Benjamin Harshav in his introduction to Herman Kruk's *The Last Days of the Jerusalem of Lithuania*,[1] as a 'major centre of a worldwide culture'.[2] The reason for this, as Harshav explains, was because of the important cultural institutions that existed in the city and the millions of Eastern European Jews that they both represented and served. Hence, Vilna was widely referred to as 'the Jerusalem of Lithuania'.[3]

In more recent history many of these institutions had been secular in outlook and character, the foremost example of which was the YIVO, the 'Yiddish Scientific Institute', founded in Vilna in 1925 as a Yiddish academy dedicated to the humanities and social sciences. However, to a large extent it was the supremely important religious figures that lived and taught in the city between the sixteenth and eighteenth centuries that led to Vilna's original rise to prominence. Foremost amongst these was the Gaon of Vilna, the 'Great One of Vilna', Rabbi Elijah ben Solomon (1720–97). This, coupled with the printing of the Vilna edition of the Talmud in the mid-nineteenth century by the Widow and Brothers Romm Publishing House, made Vilna highly important to the religious Jewish population of Eastern Europe in particular.

In September 1941, the Nazis forced all the Jews in Vilna into a ghetto, the final liquidation of which took place during September 1943. Of all the accounts that have been preserved of life in the Vilna Ghetto, by far the most extensive is that of Herman Kruk (1897–1944). Kruk was a member of the secular Bund party in Vilna, and a librarian. In the ghetto, however, his work in building and maintaining the library, containing both holy and secular books, meant that he came into close contact with all the various social groups inside the ghetto, including the religious ones. It is also apparent from his diary that he personally had a great deal of respect for the religious inhabitants of Vilna, and in particular for their literary tradition. Thus, on 7 March 1942, upon discovering that there still remained several thousand 'holy books' in the former 'Ghetto 2' that needed to be removed, Kruk remarked, 'Once again we ascertain that Vilna has been a city of learning, an inexhaustible sea'.[4] Through Kruk's references to religious life in the ghetto, we can gain some insight into both the extent of religious leadership and activity in the ghetto, as well as its significance to the inhabitants in general.

Kruk records in his diary entry for 24 April 1942 how two *yeshivot*, religious academies, had been set up in the ghetto by the 'Orthodox' population, a 'Great one' and a 'Little one'.[5] On 14 March 1942 he recorded how the 'Orthodox' had ensured that the Jews of Vilna would receive *matzah* for Passover even in the ghetto, commenting on this that, 'the world is not lawless'.[6] But most interestingly are the lengths to which the people in the ghetto as a whole, not just the religious population, went in order to maintain Jewish traditions, in particular the festivals. Kruk noted in his diary entry for 5 December 1942, when discussing the various Hanukkah celebrations that were taking place, the fact that, 'every holiday, no matter what, is enthusiastically celebrated here'.[7] Similarly, his detailed descriptions of the High Holiday celebrations in the ghetto show how important these days were to its inhabitants.[8]

On the basis of Kruk's accounts, we can therefore add another dimension to the above analysis. The preservation of Jewish religious holidays and practices was of central importance to many inhabitants of the Vilna Ghetto, and in all probability to those of other ghettos as well. But this importance was not limited to the religious inhabitants of the ghetto alone. On the contrary, it appears that many secular residents of the ghettos derived inspiration from participating in these religious occasions, led by the rabbinic leadership, perhaps as a means of identifying with their Jewish heritage in a time of extreme suffering, as well as in direct response to Nazi attempts to erase that tradition. The appropriate question to ask, therefore, is whether there were secular writers and thinkers during this period who also saw in religious life and thought a form of 'resistance' to the Nazis?

In this connection, the poems of Yitzchak Katzenelson (1886–1944) written during his time in the Warsaw Ghetto are highly illuminating. Katzenelson was a secular poet who ran a Hebrew school in Lodz before the war.[9] In 1939 he fled to Warsaw, in which he switched from the Hebrew he had written in before the war, to Yiddish, the 'language of the masses'. In the ghetto, he served as a mentor and intellectual guide to the Zionist 'Dror' youth movement, and developed a reputation, in the words of Mordechai Tenenbaum-Tamaroff (later the commander of the Jewish uprising in the Bialystok Ghetto) as a person who could take 'a bit of the desperation we were feeling and he would turn that into something that reached the skies and [through poetry] make it eternal'.[10]

One of the central themes of Katzenelson's poems was Jewish heroism and resistance of a 'spiritual' or religious nature. Two of these, both based on true stories, were preserved in the *Oyneg Shabbas* archives and the poems, together with Katzenelson's own reflections upon them, are particularly important in the context of this discussion. They provide a moving insight into rabbinical personalities who set the most extraordinary example to members of their communities, in the most tragic and extreme of circumstances.

The first of these was entitled 'The Song of Shlomo Zhelichowski'. Zhelichowski was a pious Gerer Chasid who lived in the town of Zdunska Wola. In May 1942, he was hanged together with nine other Jews in the market square. He instructed his fellow Jews that they should 'be happy' to have had the opportunity to die for the 'sanctification of the Name' (*Kiddush Hashem*). As they were led to the gallows, Zhelichowski led them in the recitation of the Neilah prayer, usually recited at the end of Yom Kippur. Katzenelson has him singing:

> Let us sing Jews! To die like a Jew, such an honour
> We are blessed. We die for our people, for the sanctification of
> the Name
> It is our great merit to hang on the gallows
> Let us sing Jews
> Let's sing a tune![11]

Kassow records, based on Katzenelson's own work, *Yidishe geto ksovim*,[12] that when he read this poem to a group of the young people of Dror, they 'reacted with puzzlement'. At a time when they were preparing for armed resistance against the Nazis, they wondered if Katzenelson was advocating 'a return to quietism and piety'. Surely, they asked, the only worthy response to the destruction was to take up arms?

Similar questions were raised in response to the second of Katzenelson's poems preserved in the Archive. This poem was entitled

'Song of the Radzyner' and was written, according to Kassow, between early July 1942 and January 1943.[13] Katzenelson read the poem aloud to members of Dror as they completed their preparations for the armed uprising that they initiated on 18 January 1943, and it was intended to serve as a, 'clarion call for leadership to restore national pride and honour'.[14] But Katzenelson's choice of theme to convey this message was unexpected.

The poem tells the story of the Chasidic Rebbe of Radzyn, Rabbi Shmuel Shlomo Leiner. Early in the war he had fled the town of Radzyn for Wlodawa, and stories of his leadership and exemplary behaviour had circulated in the Warsaw Ghetto for some time. In his poem, Katzenelson describes in detail both the Rebbe's supreme self-sacrifice and his courage in the face of Nazi persecution.[15] The Rebbe is depicted as refusing an offer to take refuge in Warsaw and instead, disguising himself as a peasant, taking a sack of money and offering the local peasants some of it in return for their assistance in helping him carry a boxcar full of dead bodies to receive a proper Jewish burial.

The point that Katzenelson wished to convey to his followers in Dror with this story, as described by Kassow, was that a Jew's task was never to 'succumb to passivity and helplessness ... to remain a Jew and remember that he had work to do', in this case the fulfilment of one of the most important commandments, that of ensuring a proper burial for the deceased.[16] In emphasizing this theme, a clear link can be discerned between Katzenelson's poem and Oshry's *Responsa From the Holocaust* cited above. As in Katzenelson's lyrical representation, Oshry describes numerous factual situations when he was called upon to rule on the best possible way of giving honour to the deceased under the circumstances. Thus, for example, on 21 September 1941, he was asked to rule on the permissibility, according to Jewish law, of using the garments of those murdered by the Nazis in the eventuality that they had been removed before their death.[17] Was this considered disrespectful? On another occasion, he was asked whether it would be permissible to eat a meal in the presence of a corpse. Ordinarily this would be forbidden under Jewish law, but in the extreme circumstances in which the removal of the body was not possible, Oshry was asked whether this could be permitted.[18]

In both instances, one from the perspective of a secular Jewish poet living in the Warsaw Ghetto and the other from a strictly Orthodox rabbi in Kovno, the message was the same. *This* was true heroism. A heroism that was uniquely Jewish, based on the values and tradition dear to them and the very spirit that the Nazis wished to eradicate. As Katzenelson put it in 'The Song of the Radzyner':

> I will sing you a song of a hero
> No, don't laugh, brothers
> how does a Jew come to sing songs of heroes?.....
>
> Gentiles ... to them belongs victory
> Only they have heroes
> They kill in war
> And destroy entire worlds.
>
> So it will be hard for me
> There is a Jew, with no weapons and no spurs
> He does not shoot
> His hands are pure, his heart is pure
> And pure is his conscience.
>
> And if this Jew spills any blood
> It is only his own
> So I am singing you a song of a hero
> But one in a very different tune.[19]

With these words, Katzenelson intended to explain to those who were puzzled by his choice of words in preparation for an armed uprising, the reason that he associated heroism with these acts of religious devotion by rabbinic leaders. Katzenelson was certainly not opposed to armed resistance. As noted by Kassow, he himself joined Dror in their January 1943 attack.[20] The Radzyner Rebbe too had reportedly told his followers to resist the Nazis by fleeing to the forests and forming partisan groups.[21] But it was clear to Katzenelson that, in the face of the might of the German army, the success of any acts of armed resistance on the part of isolated groups of Jews could only be temporary in nature. The most they could hope to achieve would be to hold the Germans at bay for a very limited period of time. Precisely at this moment, therefore, Katzenelson felt the need to remind the Jews, through his poems, 'who they had always been: a great people, to be judged not just by their fighters but also by their religious martyrs.'[22]

For writers like Katzenelson and Oshry it was clear that in order to defend their honour Jews did not have to fight 'like Poles'. For them, 'their honour was defined by a spiritual superiority that no German or Pole could take away.'[23] In this way, Katzenelson sought to restore the national pride of Polish Jewry, through his lyrical descriptions of the spiritual greatness of its religious Chasidic leadership, which he saw as both a symbol of Eastern European Jewry's spiritual vigour as well as a potent reminder of Jewish resistance and vitality. Their actions proved that 'unprecedented calamity could create extraordinary heroes.'[24]

Thus, in the Radzyner Rebbe's last words to his wife before his death at the hands of the Nazis, Katzenelson portrays him as willingly going to his death:

> 'If I could die like Rabbi Akiba, they flay me with an iron comb … don't cry … if I could have the honour – for my Jews, for God … what joy.'
>
> And he left and did not return.[25]

In these poems Katzenelson gave lyrical expression to the actions that Oshry had recorded so meticulously in Kovno. 'Resisting' the Nazis in this sense meant having the spiritual strength to face death with a head held high, proud of a strong Jewish identity and with the knowledge that the Nazis could never crush the Jewish spirit.

Conclusion

Resistance to the Nazis could take many forms. It did, of course, include the taking up of arms against the enemy. For the vast majority, however, this was either not possible, or, as Katzenelson emphasized, could only have been temporary at best in its ability to hold back the destruction of the ghettos. Under the unimaginably difficult circumstances of ghetto life, therefore, the preservation of Jewish halakhic tradition as illustrated by Oshry, the dissemination of inspirational material on matters of Jewish thought as captured in the sermons of the Piasczener Rebbe, and the attempts to preserve some semblance of the pre-war religious educational institutions and study houses were all, in a very real sense, a significant form of resistance to the Nazis. The spiritual strength shown by rabbinic leaders such as the Radzyner Rebbe also constituted resistance, not only because of his refusal, as in Katzenelson's portrayal, to act as a 'victim', but because of the inspirational example he set to both his followers and non-followers alike.

Seen in this light, the above discussion vividly illustrates the accuracy of Yehuda Bauer's assertion that, 'in opposition to a perceived German threat against the morale of the Jews, the Jewish population reacted by maintaining its cultural, educational and religious dignity.'[26] Indeed, it was this very sense of dignity, something the Nazis had tried extremely hard to eradicate through their efforts at dehumanizing the population of the ghettos, which was to some extent restored by the superhuman attempts at the preservation of a religious way of life, led by the extraordinary rabbinic personalities of the time.

In the final analysis, as Katzenelson lyrically described in his poems, it was this inner spiritual strength that granted Jews the ability to resist their oppressors. It was, perhaps, the greatest possible example of the continuity of Jewish tradition in the face of the most extreme challenge of all. And to recall the example set by these rabbinic leaders during those dark days, together with the remarkable response of their communities, remains a source of deep inspiration to this very day.

NOTES

1. Benjamin Harshav, 'Introduction', in Herman Kruk, *The Last Days of the Jerusalem of Lithuania* (New Haven, CT and London: Yale University Press, 2002).
2. Ibid., p.xxxiii.
3. Derived, according to Harshav (ibid.), from the title of the book (pub.1859) by Rashi Fin describing the history of Vilna and its Jewish community, *Kiryah Ne'emanah* – Faithful City.
4. Kruk, *The Last Days of the Jerusalem of Lithuania*, p.226.
5. Ibid., p.268.
6. Ibid., p.238.
7. Ibid., p.422.
8. See for instance, p.360.
9. Biographical data based on Samuel Kassow, *Who Will Write Our History? Rediscovering A Hidden Archive From The Warsaw Ghetto* (New York: Vintage, 2007), p.324.
10. M. Tenenbaum-Tamaroff, *Dapim min Hadleka* (Jerusalem: Hotsaat Ha-kibbutz Hameuhad, 1984), cited in ibid., pp.324–25.
11. As translated by Kassow, *Who Will Write Our History?*, p.327.
12. Yitzhak Katzenelson, *Yidishe geto ksovim*, ed. Yekhiel Shaintukh (Tel Aviv: Hotsaat Ha-Kibbutz Ha-Meuhad, 1984), p.45.
13. Kassow, *Who Will Write Our History?*, p.327.
14. Ibid.
15. Katzenelson, *Yidishe geto ksovim*, p.704.
16. Kassow, *Who Will Write Our History?*, p.329.
17. Ephraim Oshry, *Respona From The Holocaust* (New York: The Judaica Press Inc., 1983), pp.18–19.
18. Ibid., p.89.
19. Katzenelson, *Yidishe geto ksovim*, p.662.

20. Kassow, *Who Will Write Our History?*, p.330.
21. Ibid., p.328.
22. Kassow, *Who Will Write Our History?*, p.330.
23. Ibid.
24. Ibid.
25. Katzenelson, *Yidishe geto ksovim*, p.704.
26. Yehuda Bauer, *They Chose Life: Jewish Resistance in the Holocaust* (New York: Amer Jewish Committee, 1973), p.25.

Bibliography

Abramson, Henry, 'The Esh Kodesh of Rabbi Kalonimus Kalmish Shapiro: A Hasidic Treatise on Communal Trauma from the Holocaust', *Journal of Transcultural Psychiatry*, 37 (2000), pp.321–35.

Babylonian Talmud – Vilna Edition (Jerusalem: Talman Publishers, 1981).

Baer, Yitzhak, 'L'bikoret havikhuhim shel rabi Yehiel MiParis v'rabi Moshe ben Nahman' (Heb.), *Tarbiz*, 2, no.2 (1931), pp.172–87.

Bauer, Yehuda, *They Chose Life: Jewish Resistance in the Holocaust* (New York: Amer Jewish Committee, 1973).

Bauer, Yehuda, 'Interview With Yehuda Bauer – January 18th 1998'. Shoah Resource Centre, Yad Vashem, Jerusalem, http://www1.yad-vashem.org/odot.

Bogacz, Yoram, 'Genesis & The Big Bluff', *Torah Explorer*, 20 March 2012, http://torahexplorer.com/genesis-and-the-big-bluff/.

Chajes, Rabbi Zvi Hersh, *Darkhei Horaah* (Zolkiew: Meyerhoffer, 1842).

Duran, Rabbi Shimon ben Zemach, *Sheilot U'Teshuvot Tashbetz* (Jerusalem: Machon Yerushalayim, 1998 [First published Amsterdam: 1738]).

Eck, Nathan, 'Historical Research or Slander?', *Yad Vashem Studies* 6 (1967), pp.385–430.

Elon, Menachem, *Ha-Mishpat Ha-Ivri: Jewish Law: History Sources and Principles*, trans. by Bernard Auerbach and Melvin Sykes (Philadelphia, PA: Jewish Publication Society, 1994).

Epstein, Isidore (ed.), *The Soncino Talmud* (London: Soncino Press, 1935–52).

Faitelson, Alex, *Heroism and Bravery in Lithuania 1941–1945* (Jerusalem: Gefen, 1996).

Feinstein, R. Moshe, *Igrot Moshe* (New York: privately published, 1959–2011).

Feinstein, R. Moshe, *Dibrot Moshe* (Bnei Brak: 1983).

Feinstein, R. Moshe, *Darash Moshe* (New York: Mesorah Publications, 1994).

Feldstein, Steven, 'Science & Torah: Can They Go Hand In Hand?', *Intercom*, XXVI, no.1 (2006), pp.1–6.

Ferziger, Adam S., 'Religious Zealotry and Religious Law: Rethinking Conflict and Coexistence', *The Journal of Religion*, 84 (January 2004), pp.48–77.

Friedlander, R. Chaim, *Siftei Chaim. Vol. 2* (Bnei Brak: Feldheim Publishers, 1997).

Halperin, R. Dr Mordechai, *Erectile Dysfunction and Male Infertility*, Dr. Falk Schlesinger Institute for Medical-Halachic Research http://98.131.138.124/articles/FIC/20.asp, accessed 13 April 2015.

HaNagid, R. Samuel. *Introduction to the Talmud* (Jerusalem: Talman Publishers, 1981 [First published Istanbul, 1510]).

Heller, R. Yom Tov, *Tosefot Yom Tov* (Jerusalem: Horev Publishing House, 1993 [First published Cracow 1543]).

Hilberg, Raul, *The Destruction of the European Jews* (New York: Holmes & Meier, 1985 rev. edn).

Huberband, Shimon, *Kiddush Hashem: Jewish Religious and Cultural Life in Poland*, ed. and trans. by Jeffrey S. Gurock and Robert S. Hirt (New York: Ktav Publishing House Inc., 1987).

Ibn Abi Zimra, R. David, *Sh'eilot U'Teshuvot Radvaz* (Jerusalem: Walden, 1972 [First published Venice: 1749]).

Ibn Habib, R. Levi, *Sh'eilot U'teshuvot* (Venice: 1565).

Irwin-Zarecka, Iwona and Simcha Fishbane, Review of Shimon Huberband, *Kiddush Hashem: Jewish Religious and Cultural Life in Poland*, *Holocaust and Genocide Studies*, 4, no.3 (1989), pp. 382–4.

Isserlis, R. Moses, *Teshuvot Remah* (Jerusalem: Siev, 1971).

Jerusalem Talmud – Venice Edition (Jerusalem: Lebovitz-Kest, 1991).

Jewish Encyclopaedia, entry on '*Midrash Haggadah*' (New York: Funk and Wagnalls, 1906). JewishEncyclopedia.com, http://www.jewishencyclopedia.com/articles/10806-midrash-haggadah (accessed 6 August 2012).

Karelitz, R. Avraham Yeshaya, *Hazon Ish Even HaEzer* (Bnei Brak: 1991).

Karo, R. Joseph, *Kesseph Mishneh* (Commentary to Maimonides, Mishnah Torah) (Warsaw: 1880).

Kassow, Samuel, *Who Will Write Our History? Rediscovering A Hidden Archive From The Warsaw Ghetto* (New York: Vintage, 2007).

Katz, Jacob, 'Though he Sinned, he Remains an Israelite' (Heb.), *Tarbiz*, 27, no.2/3 (1957–58), pp.203–17.

Katz, Jacob, *Exclusiveness and Tolerance* (Oxford: Oxford University Press, 1961).

Katz, Jacob, 'Orthodoxy in Historical Perspective', *Studies in Contemporary Jewry*, 2 (1986), pp.3–17.

Katz, Jacob, *The Shabbes Goy: A Study in Halakhic Flexibility* (Philadelphia, PA: Jewish Publication Society, 1989).

Katz, Jacob, *A House Divided* (Hanover, NH: Brandeis University Press, 1998).

Katzenelson, Yitzhak, *Yidishe geto ksovim*, ed. Yekhiel Shaintukh (Tel Aviv: Hotsaat Ha-Kibbutz Ha-Meuhad, 1984).

Krochmal, R. Menahem Mendel ben R. Abraham, *Responsa Zemah Zedek* (Jerusalem: Wagshal, 1982 [First published Altdorf: 1775]).

Kruk, Herman, *The Last Days of the Jerusalem of Lithuania* (ed. Benjamin Harshav) (New Haven, CT and London: Yale University Press, 2002).

Lamm, R. Norman. 'The Religious Implication of Extra-terrestrial Life', in A. Carmell and C. Domb (eds), *Challenge: Torah Views on Science and Its Problems* (New York: Feldheim Publishers, 1978), pp.354–98.

Landau, R. Judah, *Responsa Nodah Bi'Yehuda, Mahadura Kamma* (Warsaw: 1880, 1st edn).

Lowe, R. Judah, *Sefer Gevurot Hashem* (New York: Judaica Press, 1969).

Lowe, R. Judah, *Baer HaGolah* (Israel: Books Export Enterprises Ltd, 1980).

Lowe, R. Judah, *Netivot Olam, Netiv Hatorah* (Bnei Brak: Yahadut Publications, 1980).

Luzzatto, R. Moses Hayyim, *Maamar Al Hahaggadot* (Essay on the Aggadah) (Warsaw: Ahavah Publications, 1936).

Maccoby, Hyam, *Judaism on Trial: Jewish-Christian Disputations in the Middle Ages* (London: Littman Library of Jewish Civilisation, 1993).

Maimonides, R. Moshe, *Guide For the Perplexed*, trans. M. Friedlander (London: Routledge & Kegan Paul Ltd, 1904).

Maimonides, R. Moshe, *Commentary on the Mishnah* (Jerusalem: Mossad HaRav Kook, 1963–67).

Maimonides, R. Moshe, *Mishneh Torah*, trans. Eliyahu Touger (New York: Moznaim Publishers, 1997).

Marrus, Michael, *The Holocaust in History* (New York: Meridian, 1987).

Novak, David, 'Modern Responsa: 1800 to the Present', in N.S. Hecht, B.S. Jackson, S.M. Passamaneck, D. Piattelli and A.M. Rabello (eds), *An Introduction to the History and Sources of Jewish Law* (New York: Oxford University Press, 1996), pp.380–95.

Oshry, Ephraim, *Respona From The Holocaust* (New York: The Judaica Press Inc., 1983).

Oshry, Ephraim, *Sheilot Utshuvot Mima'amakim* (Heb. 5 vols) (New York: Modern Linotype Co., 1959–79).

Oshry, Ephraim, *The Annihilation of Lithuanian Jewry* (New York: The Judaica Press Inc., 1995).

Polen, Nehemia, *The Holy Fire, the Teachings of Rabbi Kalonymus Kalman Shapira, the Rebbe of the Warsaw Ghetto* (Maryland: Jason Aronson, 1994).

Prager, Moshe, *Those Who Never Yielded* (Wisconsin: Lightbooks, 1980).

Ruderman, David B., *Jewish Thought and Scientific Discovery in Early Modern Europe* (New Haven, CT: Yale University Press, 1995).

Sacks, Jonathan, *One People?* (London: Littman Library of Jewish Civilisation, 1993).

Sacks, Jonathan, 'Fashioning the World Anew with Winged Thoughts', http://www.rabbisacks.org/fashioning-world-anew-winged-thoughts/, accessed 20 April 2015 (first published in *The Times*, 21 November 2008).

Samet, Moshe, 'The Beginnings of Orthodoxy', *Modern Judaism* 8, no.3 (1988), pp.249–69.

Schlesinger, Akiva Yoseph, *Na'ar Ha'Ivri* (Vienna: 1863).

Schlesinger, Akiva Yoseph, *Lev Ha'Ivri* (Lemberg: Goldberg, 1873).

Schneersohn, R. Menachem M., 'A Letter on Science and Judaism', in A. Carmell and C. Domb (eds), *Challenge: Torah Views on Science and Its Problems* (New York: Feldheim Publishers, 1978), pp.142–9.

Schneider, Israel, 'Jewish Law and Copyright', *Journal of Halacha and Contemporary Society*, 21 (1991), pp.84–96.

Schorr, R. Yisroel Simcha (ed.), *Schottenstein Edition Talmud Bechoros Vol.2.* (New York: Artscroll Mesorah Publications, 2003).

Schroeder, Gerald L., *Genesis and the Big Bang* (New York: Bantam, 1990).

Shapira, R. Chayyim Elazar, *Responsa Minchat Elazar* (Jerusalem: Ohr Torah Munkatzch, 1996).

Shapiro, Kalonymus Kalman, *Eish Kodesh* (Jerusalem: Feldheim Publishers, 2007, rev. edn).

Silber, Michael, 'The Emergence of Ultra-Orthodoxy – The Invention of a Tradition', in Jack Wertheimer (ed.), *The Uses of Tradition* (New York: Jewish Theological Seminary of America, 1992), pp.23–84.

Silber, Michael, 'Alliance of the Hebrews, 1863–1875: The Diaspora Roots of an Ultra-Orthodox Proto-Zionist Utopia in Palestine', *Journal of Israeli History: Politics, Society, Culture*, 27, no.2 (2008), pp.119–47.

Sirkis, R. Joel, *Bayyit Hadash (BaH)* (Jerusalem: Machon Yerushalayim, 1993–94 [First published Cracow: 1631–39]).

Sloan, Jacob (ed. and trans.), *Notes From The Warsaw Ghetto: The Journal of Emmanuel Ringleblum* (New York: Schocken, 1986).

Sofer, R. Moses, *Chiddushei Chatam Sofer* (Mihalevitz: Greenfeld Publishing, 1928).

Sofer, R. Moses, *Chatam Sofer Al Chamisha Chumshei Torah* (Mihalevitz: Greenfeld Publishing, 1928).

Sofer, R. Moses, *Sheilot U'Teshuvot Chatam Sofer* (Jerusalem: Machon L'Hotza'at Sefarim V'Cheker Kitvei Yad Al Shem HaChatam Sofer, 2008 [First published Pressburg, Bratislava: Anton Schmidt Printing Press, 1859]).

Sterling, Eric, 'Review of *The Annihilation of Lithuanian Jewry*', *Journal of Holocaust and Genocide Studies*, 12 (1998), pp.158–61.

Tenenbaum-Tamaroff, Mordechai, *Dapim min Hadleka* (Jerusalem: Hotsaat Ha-Kibbutz Ha-Meuhad, 1984).

Teshuvot Rashi (New York: Israel Elfenbein, 1943).

Walldenberg, R. Eliezer, *Responsa Tzitz Eliezer* (Jerusalem: Bloom, 1945–1996).

Weinberg, Joanna, *Azariah de' Rossi, The Light of the Eyes* (New Haven, CT: Yale University Press, 2001).

Yekutiel, R. Meir ben, *Haggahot Maimoniot L'Sefer Nashim* (Jerusalem: Hotzaat Shabse Frankel, 1972).

Thank you for reading this Vallentine Mitchell Publishers book.

Vallentine Mitchell serves both the academic community and the educated lay-reader, and promotes learning and scholarship to a global audience. Our staff is committed to publishing to the highest standards across a range of disciplines of interest to the Jewish and wider community in the Humanities and Social Sciences. We support authors through strong editorial, marketing and production skills, and are committed to serving international scholarship by promoting our authors' writing and research so that they make the maximum impact on, and gain the widest possible, readership.

Vallentine Mitchell's publishing programme primarily covers Jewish History, Culture and Heritage; Jewish Thought; Middle Eastern History, Politics and Culture; Religion and the Holocaust.

Full details of our publishing programme can be found at our website:

www.vmbooks.com

E-books are available via Ebrary and ProQuest and from mid 2017 via our website